# 2002
# WAYS
# TO SAY
## *"I love you"*

# 2002
# WAYS
# TO SAY
# "I love you"

**Cyndi Haynes
&
Dale Edwards**

Adams Media Corporation
Holbrook, Massachusetts

Published by Adams Media Corporation
260 Center Street
Holbrook, MA 02343

ISBN: 1-55850-437-0

Printed in the United States of America.

J I H G F E D C B A

*This book is available at quantity discounts for bulk purchases.*
*For information, call 1-800-872-5627.*

1. Drift away while listening to soft, romantic music together.

2. Send a gigantic greeting card.

3. Add a special touch to breakfast in bed by placing a flower on the tray.

4. Recreate your first date.

5. Express your true feelings on a banner.

6. Throw a gala in your loved one's honor.

7. Hold hands while watching television.

8. For a touch of romance, keep a candle on the night stand.

9. Spend an afternoon taking her shopping.

10. Purchase an addition to his collection.

11. Start your own traditions.

12. Dine by candlelight.

13. Rent a Rolls Royce to cruise around town

14. Plant flowers at her home.

15. Delight in the romance of *Romeo and Juliet*

16. Hug.

17. Visit his hometown.

18. Gaze into each other's eyes.

19. Go a little ape and spend the night together in a tree house.

20. Pull your mattress onto the fire escape to enjoy the night under the stars.

21. Attend religious services together.

22. Kiss hello.

23. Tuck a love note in his briefcase.

24. Call when you are out of town.

25. Change the oil in her car.

26. Bring her candy.

27. Compile a scrapbook of your times together.

28. Give away the key to your heart.

29. Always be kind to your loved one's friends.

30. Be the first one to say, "I love you."

31. Hire a skywriter.

32. Prepare his favorite meal.

33. Dine on your fine china.

34. Sleep in your sleeping bag beside his bed when he is ill so that you can nurse him back to health.

35. Bathe her dog.

36. Cut a loving message in the front yard with your lawn mower.

37. Plant a tree on the anniversary of when you first met.

38. Find a long lost childhood friend of your mate.

39. Attend a family reunion in good spirits.

40. Spell out your feelings in a bowl of alphabet soup.

41. Share a bubble bath.

42. Knit him a sweater.

43. Give her a fabulous piece of jewelry.

44. Steal a kiss in a public place.

45. Pamper him with an old fashioned barber shop shave.

46. Carry home her twenty-five-pound bag of dog food for her four-legged baby.

47. Give a subscription to a favorite magazine.

48. Remember to celebrate Sweetest Day every October.

---

*Friendship is one mind in two bodies.*
    —MENCIUS

---

49. Make up your own private nicknames.

50. Put snow tires on her car.

51. Pitch in and help him address holiday cards.

52. Share the writings of Elizabeth Barret Browning.

53. Never make fun of her hair on a "bad hair day."

54. Send a romantic fax.

55. Spell "I love you" with pepperoni on your next pizza.

56. Rent *Sleepless in Seattle*.

57. Wear his favorite perfume.

58. Buy him a pair of silk boxers.

59. Always shake hands with her dad.

60. Entertain his family on holidays.

61. Give him cooking lessons.

62. Propose on bended knee

63. Redecorate his office.

64. Be cheerful.

65. Help type his report.

66. Cultivate joint friendships.

67. Make time for a quick lunch during a hectic day.

68. Furnish her with your voice mail number.

69. Tidy up his apartment.

70. Take his temperature when he is sick.

71. Create your own holidays.

72. Leave a fun message on his answering machine.

73. Videotape his ball game.

74. Surprise her by returning her car with a full tank of gas.

75. Knit booties for his new niece or nephew.

76. Have a date every week with each other.

77. Burglarproof her place.

78. Sort his socks.

79. Pass love notes discreetly in public.

> *A man should keep his friendships in constant repair.*
> —SAMUEL JOHNSON

80. Always be loyal.

81. Pitch in and help him address Christmas cards.

82. Make sure he gets his flu shot before the cold season begins.

83. Laugh *with* each other (not *at* each other).

84. Send a Valentine's Day card in the summer.

85. Be the first to say that you're sorry.

86. Forget about all of your old loves.

87. Spend the entire day in bed.

88. Help him choose his wardrobe.

89. Clean out her garage.

90. Massage your mate's tired feet.

91. Plant a rose garden for her.

92. Fluff her pillow.

93. Baby-sit his nieces and nephews.

94. Don't borrow without asking for permission.

95. Practice safe sex.

96. Insist that he buckle his seat belt.

97. Carry her luggage after a long trip.

98. Hide a love note in a public place where she will be sure to find it.

99. Lend money in a pinch.

100. Help out his favorite charity

101. Build an elaborate doghouse for her puppy

102. Have your sister ask her to be a bridesmaid in her wedding

103. Remember birthdays.

104. Know his clothing size

105. Make the bed.

106. Write love poems.

107. Cut his hair.

108. Play "your song" on the jukebox

---

Three of the most important words in any language:
*"I love you."*

---

109. Plan a special homecoming for his return.

110. Buy an antique bed with a romantic past.

111. Make plans for your future together.

112. Treat her to a pedicure.

113. Get tested for AIDS.

114. Send your mate a fan letter.

115. Purchase flowers from a street vendor.

116. Teach his dog a new trick.

117. Toast each other with a fine glass of wine.

118. Hide an expensive, little gift in a box of Cracker Jacks.

119. Play a love song on your harmonica.

120. Treat her to a box of scented soaps for a luxurious, relaxing bath.

121. Put marshmallows in his hot chocolate.

122. Tote her on your bike.

123. Dramatically express your feelings for all time in a stained glass window.

124. Chase rainbows together.

125. Play footsies.

126. Talk for hours on the phone.

127. Paint your message on the freshly fallen snow.

128. Always make your lover feel special.

129. Count to ten before you start an argument.

130. Set off your own fireworks on the Fourth of July.

131. Be enthusiastic about her accomplishments.

132. Roll all of his loose pennies.

133. Toss coins into a wishing well together.

134. Send a Thanksgiving Day card that says she is one of your biggest blessings.

135. Never put his name on a chain letter.

136. Have a standing Saturday night date.

137. Watch the same television programs even when you are apart.

138. Be generous with your time.

139. Give her your mom's best recipes.

---

*Faith is love taking the form of aspiration.*
—WILLIAM E. CHANNING

---

140. Buy him a mustache grooming kit.

141. Allow yourself to fall madly in love.

142. Shovel her sidewalk after a big snow.

143. Make a romantic wish on a new moon.

144. Relax while having a fireside chat.

145. Express your true feelings on a T-shirt.

146. Purchase a gift from Saks Fifth Avenue.

147. Be patient.

148. Embroider a loving message on his pillowcase.

149. Share your box of Godiva chocolates.

150. Keep each other warm with body heat.

151. Share breath mints.

152. Ask him out first.

153. Have a song dedicated to her on the radio.

154. Act on your spur of the moment urge to go on a getaway weekend.

155. Shampoo her rug.

156. Place a pearl in an oyster for her to find.

157. Be lazy together.

158. Keep the love light burning for each other.

159. Spend an entire day communicating through touch, not words.

160. Make sure she gets plenty of rest.

161. Wear matching robes to breakfast.

162. Have a child together.

163. Dedicate a book to your mate.

164. Laugh at his old jokes.

165. Take time off from work just to be together.

166. Bake him homemade croissants for breakfast.

167. Help her shake the winter blues.

168. Buy animal crackers for him when you do the grocery shopping.

169. Share an all day sucker.

170. Decorate his bachelor pad.

171. Create a signal for silence when you need to have quiet time.

172. Help run errands.

173. Make arrangements to have the waiter sing "Happy Birthday."

174. Call him on his car phone just to say "drive carefully."

175. Play a fun prank.

176. Type his resumé.

177. Discover your own secret hideaway.

178. Bury her in fall leaves.
179. Spend the day free from distractions.
180. Exchange romantic ideas.
181. Have the band play "your song" at a park concert.
182. Always dine at romantic tables for two.
183. Organize his clothes closet.
184. Frame his awards.
185. Whisper in bed.
186. Fall asleep touching.
187. Always try to put the other person first.
188. Send yellow roses for friendship along with some red roses to show all sides to your relationship.
189. The next time a great romantic song comes on the radio, tell her it reminds you of her.
190. Do a favor for his mom.
191. Design your dream home together.
192. Spend a Saturday morning dozing side by side.
193. Save all of his letters.
194. Look at the world through your partner's eyes.
195. Bake a fabulous birthday cake.
196. Tuck each other into bed.
197. Send messages in Morse Code.
198. Create a shared history.

**199.** Refrain from using guilt to get your way.

**200.** Start a joint savings account.

**201.** Enjoy whipped cream and strawberries at night.

**202.** Remain friends during hard times.

**203.** Place "SWAK" on all your envelopes.

**204.** Dance the night away to romantic music.

**205.** Create your own "love coupons."

**206.** Save your biggest smile for her.

---

Reasons to Write a Thank You Note:
*gifts*
*help with a project*
*a loan*
*hospitality*
*advice*
*special kindness*
*favors*

---

**207.** Stay in the bridal suite when you travel.

**208.** Accept compliments gracefully.

**209.** Pose for pictures together.

**210.** Make each other late for work.

**211.** Order chateaubriand for two.

**212.** Place a penny in his new wallet for luck.

213. Feed each other fabulous finger food.

214. Sing in the shower together.

215. Be sweethearts for life.

216. Let him choose the topping for the pizza.

217. Rent a piece of extravagant jewelry for her to wear on a special night.

218. Tell your partner that you think that they are sexy.

219. Hide a piece of jewelry in an ice cube for her to find.

220. Indulge his sweet tooth.

221. Rent a country cottage for the weekend.

222. Never use the excuse that you have a headache.

223. Say something kind everyday.

224. Reread your marriage vows.

225. Write an unexpected letter of appreciation.

226. Use good table manners.

227. Do something off of his "To Do" list.

228. Be willing to make small sacrifices for your relationship.

229. Scratch his itch.

230. Provide each other with a relationship warranty.

231. Zip up her dress for her.

232. Make the quality of your relationship a top priority.

233. Create a home, not just a house to live in.

234. Wear your wedding ring at all times.

235. Celebrate the fact that you are a couple.

236. Learn to read her mind.

237. Watch the DeBeer's diamond ads together.

238. Try to be sexy in his eyes.

239. Kiss every time the clock chimes during the next twenty-four hours.

240. Know her ring size.

241. Hold good thoughts about her at all times.

242. Install a dimmer switch in your bedroom.

243. Allow her to see you cry.

244. Brush her hair.

245. Say "Yes"!

246. Give an old fashioned identity bracelet.

247. Sign a cast with a special sentiment.

248. Smooch at the drive-in movie.

249. Offer praise often in public.

250. Buy a hope chest and fill it together.

251. Treat him like Prince Charming.

252. Kiss a wound to make it feel better.

253. Keep secrets.

254. Serenade him.

255. Share your innermost feelings under the cover of darkness.

256. Treat her to something new and exciting to wear.

257. Hire a limousine.

258. Take her to one of America's most charming towns, Carmel, California, for a romantic weekend getaway.

259. Read between the lines when he is sad

260. After a trip abroad, wait for her to make it through customs.

261. Keep the candy jar on her desk full.

262. Have his and her pets when you like cats and he likes dogs.

263. Place lamps on both sides of the bed so you can read while not keeping the other awake.

264. Encourage him to be rid of inhibitions.

265. Value her opinion.

266. Take her needs seriously.

267. Tell him you want a "Mrs." before your name.

268. Share life's risks.

269. Practice making the best of things.

270. Call to check on him when he is sick.

271. Cry at the same time during a sad movie.

272. Get to know the real person.

273. Do the dishes after the other person prepares the meal.

274. Make love on the beach.

275. Give her the prize that you've just won.

276. Rekindle the flame.

277. Dance at home to the radio.

278. Stroll hand in hand in a summer shower.

279. Purchase matching coffee mugs.

280. Smile when you think about each other.

281. Look forward to being together.

282. Hold hands during a wedding ceremony.

283. Wake him up when he is having a nightmare.

284. Clip out "Cathy" comics that relate to your relationship.

285. Keep a joint diary.

286. Be persistent in your love.

287. Share a lap desk.

288. Make your apartment feel like a home.

289. Put your feelings on a button.

290. Use the same body language patterns.

291. Research her family tree.

292. Help him keep in touch with distant relatives.

293. Ask your mom to knit her a great sweater.

294. Help remember doctor's appointments for him.

295. Role play in preparation for a job interview.

296. Have her favorite appetizers waiting when she gets home from work.

297. Prepare a cozy meal for two.

Traditional Anniversary Gifts:
*First–Paper*
*Fifth–Wood*
*Tenth–Tin*
*Fifteenth–Crystal*
*Twentieth–China*
*Twenty-fifth–Silver*
*Thirtieth–Pearl*
*Fortieth–Ruby*
*Fiftieth–Gold*

**298.** During bad weather, keep an ear tuned to the weather reports to learn about current driving conditions for him.

**299.** Put snow tires on her car.

**300.** Dress alike on Halloween.

**301.** Celebrate "Spouse Appreciation Day."

**302.** Keep his baby pictures in a special place

**303.** Propose all over again.

**304.** Fix chicken noodle soup when she is sick

**305.** Give her anything in 24kt. gold.

**306.** Provide a sympathetic ear.

**307.** Towel dry her hair.

**308.** Keep your promises.

**309.** Lay an orchid on her pillow.

310. Call her an angel.

311. Pretend to like sports for his sake.

312. Pull the shades down. . . .

313. Car pool just so you can spend more time together.

314. Touch constantly.

315. Make her a June bride.

316. Tickle each other gently.

317. Get in the habit of doing small favors for each other on a regular basis.

318. Make room in your closet for her stuff.

319. Use lace tablecloths and napkins.

320. Be mesmerized by her beauty.

321. Have the waiter bring her a flower.

322. Always look for the best in each other.

323. Spend the evening propped up on floor pillows.

324. Keep your sense of humor in bed.

325. Clean out her cat's litter box.

326. Feed the parking meter so that he won't get a ticket.

327. Go to bed early and share a new novel.

328. Say "ours" instead of "mine."

329. Hide a love note that may not be found for months.

330. Give her your college ring (even if you graduated years ago).

331. Duplicate his key so that you will have one.

332. Take a picnic feast to your hotel room.

333. Plan a romantic scavenger hunt.

334. Give him all of the green M&Ms.

335. Be tender.

336. Spend hours in front of a dying fire.

337. Make sure that she takes her vitamins.

338. Write your love letters on expensive writing paper.

339. Have your feelings announced on a police car's loud speaker.

340. Admit your feelings.

341. Give her a solitaire.

342. Walk arm in arm.

343. Know that you will never love anyone else like this.

344. Call her on an in-flight phone.

345. Travel to the ends of the earth together.

346. Needlepoint a cover for a brick from the first home that you live in together.

347. Bronze your baby shoes side by side.

348. Send her an arrangement like her mother's bridal bouquet.

349. Give her a gumball machine ring as a down payment on a more promising one.

350. Have tons of new beginnings.

351. Get a romantic license plate.

**352.** Send a greeting card everyday for a month.

**353.** Ask her for the next dance.

**354.** Wear French lingerie.

---

*The manner of giving shows the character of the giver more than the gift itself.*
—JOHANN KASPAR LAVATER

---

**355.** Rock her to sleep in your arms.

**356.** Draw hearts on all your notes.

**357.** Use him as a big pillow.

**358.** Kiss under the boardwalk.

**359.** Serve caviar and champagne.

**360.** Learn to verbalize your feelings.

**361.** Send flowers on the first day of each new season.

**362.** Make brief calls to her at work.

**363.** Put his number on a speed dial button on your phone (in the number one spot, of course).

**364.** Send a thank-you note after a great evening.

**365.** Put forth the maximum effort in your relationship.

**366.** Call when you are going to be late.

**367.** Eat dessert first.

**368.** Pillow fight.

**369.** Introduce your parents to his parents.

**370.** Kiss her hand.

**371.** Put her name on your life insurance policy.

**372.** Compose a love song.

**373.** Act like a couple at parties.

**374.** Talk to her while you watch the ball game.

**375.** Order a massage for two.

**376.** Have a romantic picnic on the roof.

**377.** Write to Santa together.

**378.** Visit her family.

**379.** Give each other a facial.

**380.** Read religious books together.

**381.** Send a card to someone special from his past, such as a teacher or playmate.

**382.** Sleep under the Christmas tree on Christmas Eve.

**383.** Tell a romantic bedtime story.

**384.** Decorate for the holidays.

**385.** Hide a beautiful nightgown under her pillow for her to find.

**386.** Fix freshly squeezed orange juice for breakfast.

**387.** Send cookies in the mail.

**388.** Grill her steak exactly the way she likes it.

**389.** Smooch in a phone booth in between making calls.

**390.** Send a card when it is least expected.

> *He gives double who gives unasked.*
> —ARAB PROVERB

391. Stand up when she enters the room.

392. Buy a music box that plays "your song."

393. Be the first to accept an invitation to her party.

394. Share your good news with each other first, before you tell others.

395. Send her flowers when her girlfriends get married.

396. Clean out his car the day before his boss will be riding in it

397. Enlarge your best photograph of him and send it to his mom.

398. Make each other's friends feel welcomed.

399. Scheme together.

400. Wink at each other.

401. Put a tool kit in her car.

402. Set the alarm clock for when he needs to get up.

403. Play classical music to set the mood for a great evening.

404. Kiss away her tears.

405. Shine his shoes.

406. Call in sick for her.

**407.** Practice M.Y.O.B. (minding your own business) when it comes to his family.

**408.** If she loves teddy bears, treat her to a stay at the White Swan Inn in San Francisco.

**409.** Promise forever.

**410.** View the Northern Lights.

**411.** Throw a big party for every milestone birthday.

**412.** Collect things for your dream home together.

**413.** Work at being a great couple.

**414.** Put cinnamon sticks in his apple cider.

**415.** Make a fuss over her successes.

**416.** Look your best for him.

**417.** Set off fireworks on your anniversary.

**418.** Live by the Golden Rule.

**419.** Take an evening carriage ride.

**420.** Sign your letters with x's and o's.

**421.** Meet for a champagne brunch.

**422.** Leave her a secret message.

**423.** Put much thought into your gift giving.

**424.** Hurry home from work just to be in each other's arms.

**425.** Give her your books of trading stamps to buy what she wants.

**426.** Start a collection for her.

**427.** Take pictures of the important moments of her life.

**428.** Give him your lucky penny.

---

*What is a true gift? One for which nothing is expected in return.*

—CONFUCIUS

---

**429.** Share your bounty after shopping at a bulk grocery store.

**430.** Celebrate all red letter days that are important to him.

**431.** Kiss and make up after a fight.

**432.** Buy ID tags for her pets.

**433.** Vote for him when he is running for office.

**434.** Go to bed before you are both tired.

**435.** Dance by moonlight.

**436.** Make a memory file.

**437.** Purchase a candelabra for properly setting the mood.

**438.** Quote her favorite author back to her.

**439.** Make honesty your policy.

**440.** Give him the window seat on the plane.

**441.** Present more than one gift on all holidays on which you exchange presents.

**442.** Pass on all second hand compliments.

**443.** Fix gourmet provisions for his camping trip.

**444.** Slip satin slippers on her feet after a long day.

**445.** Let her have the last word (at least once in awhile).

**446.** Back his cause.

**447.** Cut down on sodium in his diet.

**448.** Hang a "Home Sweet Home" sign where you live.

**449.** If she loves to be in the kitchen, give her a vintage apron.

**450.** Plug in nightlights all over her new apartment.

**451.** Give gag gifts for no special occasion.

**452.** Frame a photo of her pooch for her office.

**453.** When you dine at a Japanese restaurant always ask for one of the private dining rooms for the two of you.

**454.** Collect your easiest recipes and give them to him.

**455.** Make a cassette tape of a concert you attended together.

**456.** Revert to childhood and play spin the bottle.

**457.** Pretend to be snowed in for the weekend, even during a heat wave.

**458.** Host a birthday bash for her pet.

**459.** Have a last fling of the summer with each other.

**460.** Throw a late night pool party for two.

**461.** Present her with a beautiful bride doll.

**462.** Leave the tip when she pays for dinner.

463. Help him get accepted for membership to your club.

464. Become friends with his friends.

465. Spend the night in his childhood home.

466. Give him lawn care service for a year.

467. Name your boat after her.

468. Purchase romantic bedding.

469. Send a gift inside a balloon.

470. Remodel her bathroom.

471. Send a daily get well card when your mate is sick.

472. Make the winning bid on an item she loves at an auction.

473. Install a car alarm in his new car.

474. Invest in a porch swing to encourage late night chats.

475. Defrost his refrigerator.

---

*Love is the only commodity that power cannot command and money cannot buy.*
—ANONYMOUS

---

476. Give her a plane ticket to visit her family.

477. Consider becoming foster parents together.

478. Clean out her gutters.

479. Never steal the covers.

**480.** Curl up together.

**481.** Caress each other.

**482.** Have a "future evening" where you make predictions about your relationship.

**483.** Surprise him with twenty-six gifts from A to Z that begin with each of the letters of the alphabet.

**484.** Sleep in his shirt or pajama top.

**485.** Find a keychain that reveals your true feelings.

**486.** Mail a yardstick for her to measure how her feelings for you have grown.

**487.** Hire a builder to build him his own think tank.

**488.** Commission an artist to paint her portrait

**489.** Give her secretary flowers to place on her desk before she gets to work.

**490.** Send a bouquet of miniature roses to let him know that it is the small things in life that really count.

**491.** Count your joint blessings.

**492.** When ice is on her windshield, scrape it off in a heart shape.

**493.** Dine at a fabulous French restaurant.

**494.** Remind all of her friends to send her a card on her birthday.

**495.** Be attentive to your mate's needs.

496. When his budget is tight, suggest a dutch-treat date.

497. Inscribe a book with a loving message.

498. Get her favorite munchies at the movies.

499. Escort her home.

500. Always be true blue.

501. Place a flashing neon sign in his front yard declaring your feelings.

502. Give his dog a fun nickname.

503. Attend a religious class or seminar together.

504. Install a burglar alarm.

505. Insist that she get an annual mammogram.

506. Buy her a gold coin from the year you met.

---

Ingredients Inherent to Great
Romantic Moments:
*The unexpected*
*Tension*
*Surprise*
*The illicit*
*Mystery*
*Uncertainty*

---

507. If he is in the public eye, hire a clipping bureau for him.

508. Pick up his shirts at the cleaners.

**509.** Win her a prize at a carnival.

**510.** Memorize her speech so you can coach her from the audience if she becomes nervous or forgetful.

**511.** Chop firewood for her.

**512.** Always treat your mate as your lover.

**513.** Flirt with each other constantly.

**514.** Be the first to jump out of bed to make the coffee in the morning.

**515.** Give the gift of lessons.

**516.** Treat yourselves to a hot tub in your home.

**517.** Be adventurous with a home cooked ethnic meal from your mate's background.

**518.** Write name tags for all of his family and office holiday gifts.

**519.** Hunt through holiday catalogues in search of the perfect gift.

**520.** Place your picture in his wallet.

**521.** Recycle by sending her favorite love notes again and again.

**522.** Model a gingerbread house after your dream home.

**523.** Help her clean out her closets.

**524.** Tie his tie.

**525.** Put an ad on local television expressing your love for her.

**526.** Clean up her old, muddy tennis shoes.

527. Relive your best date again and again.
528. Create your own special magic.
529. Match up his friends with your friends.
530. Send a small evergreen tree with a note stating that you are pining for him.
531. Fly a heart-shaped kite.
532. Give him a medal for being the very best.
533. Blow kisses.
534. Hold hands in public.
535. Kidnap him for a breakfast surprise.
536. Preserve a time capsule of your relationship.
537. Decorate his dog's house for the holidays.
538. Take dance lessons together.
539. Prepare heart-shaped pancakes for breakfast.
540. Label all of her VCR tapes.

---

*Those who love deeply never grow old.*
—ANONYMOUS

---

541. Host a pajama party for two.
542. Return to the scene of your first kiss.
543. Compose lyrics to "your song."
544. Make her "Queen for the Day."
545. Workout together.
546. Toast each other at the dinner table.

547. Eat junk food by candlelight.

548. Squeeze his hand during the scary part of a movie.

549. Call often.

550. Make time for dating.

551. Encourage spiritual growth.

552. Switch the place cards at dinner just so you can sit together.

553. Help out in the kitchen.

554. Send flowers the day before her next party.

555. Write "I love you" on the top of the butter with a toothpick.

556. Decorate the holiday cookies she bakes.

557. Treat her to a week at a spa.

558. Write a rhyme about your relationship.

559. Buy her one of her favorite perfumes.

560. Send two bouquets instead of one.

561. Dance cheek to cheek.

562. Donate blood when he is going to have an operation

563. Work a heart-shaped puzzle together.

564. Write your own wedding vows.

565. Present her with your grandmother's engagement ring.

566. Return his calls promptly.

567. Kiss at midnight on New Year's Eve.

568. Elope.

569. Tuck a love note in her robe.

570. Give him an engagement gift.

571. Place a rose inside her morning paper.

572. Pay back any money that you owe.

573. Get the tape of the best episode of his favorite show.

574. Create a family tree together.

575. Entertain her friends in grand style.

576. Create you own rituals.

577. Plan a hay ride for two.

578. Host a mixed doubles tournament on Valentine's Day.

579. Send a heart-shaped Waterford crystal paperweight to her at the office.

580. Invite her over for breakfast.

581. Serve a midnight dinner by candlelight.

582. Bake a sweetheart cake.

583. Offer to share the driving on long road trips.

584. Gladly tune in the home shopping channel and help her watch for bargains on a Saturday afternoon

585. Play a romantic joke on April Fool's Day.

586. Inquire about what she wants for her birthday.

587. Needlepoint a heart pillow for your bed.

588. Take a second honeymoon.

589. Take a third honeymoon.

590. Learn to give a great back massage.

591. Return his overdue library books.

592. Bombard her with tons of love letters.

593. Throw an un-birthday party.

594. Have the ringmaster express your feelings during the circus.

595. Write lengthy love letters.

596. Stage your own kissing marathon.

597. Send a singing telegram.

598. Wrap your gifts in wedding paper just to be romantic.

599. Hire a limousine to take you on a romantic Christmas-time ride around town to see the lights.

600. Be playful with each other.

601. Invite him in for a nightcap after a great date.

602. Learn to waltz.

603. Play the romantic music of Johnny Mathis.

604. Share your fantasies.

605. Always give gifts in person.

606. Burn perfumed candles.

607. Help her on and off with her coat.

608. Only break a date in the case of an emergency.

609. Tuck a love note in his suitcase when he is going away on a business trip.

---

The Meaning of Roses:
*Pink – affection*
*White – purity*
*Yellow – friendship*
*Red – love & romance*

---

610. Help entertain his business associates.

611. Enjoy a picnic among fountains in an urban plaza setting.

612. Have an afternoon tea together at a fine hotel.

613. Beautifully wrap all gifts.

614. Fingerpaint a romantic masterpiece together.

615. Be sentimental when it comes to your relationship.

616. Put effort into planning your dates.

617. Bat your eyelashes at him.

618. Send him a drink in a restaurant when he doesn't know that you are there.

619. Throw away your little black book.

620. Agree to disagree.

621. Be a secret pal.

622. Give books of romantic poetry.

623. Fill her car with balloons.

624. Hang mistletoe in June (and put it to use).

625. Send her a bottle of pink champagne and a dozen pink roses.

626. Give a four leaf clover on the eve of a big event for good luck.

627. Send a Mylar balloon.

628. Place red Christmas lights on plants for February 14th.

629. Make a cookie bouquet out of heart-shaped cookies.

630. Hang posters of famous romantic couples.

631. Validate each other's feelings.

632. Find out about places she would like to go and take her there.

633. Take a moonlit walk on Sunday to start the week off right.

634. Treat her to a shopping spree at a lingerie shop.

635. Take a mid-week mini vacation.

636. Snuggle often.

637. Help him pick out his ties.

638. Learn all the intricate rules of his favorite sport.

639. Keep an eye on her blue chip stock.

640. Carry groceries home for her.

641. Be respectful.

642. Cultivate trust by always being honest.

643. Treat him to a night at a romantic inn.

644. Play chauffeur with your four wheel drive after a major snow storm

645. Encourage him to have regular check-ups.

646. Cheer for him at a sporting event

647. Make a romantic quilt that expresses your love

648. Give her a heart pendant

649. Smile at each other.

650. Listen with your heart as well as your head.

651. Browse through old photos of the two of you

652. Go to lunch with his best friend to learn more about him.

653. Feed her pet when she is out of town.

654. Speak kindly about her family.

655. Pray together.

656. Make a practice of long kisses.

657. Bake gourmet brownies.

658. Compliment her new hair style

659. Help him stick to his diet.

660. Wash her car.

661. Pitch in and help with extra work at the office.

662. Rent her favorite movie.

663. Bring a beautiful rose to your love.

664. Decorate his apartment for the holidays.

665. Give him a gift certificate to his favorite restaurant.

666. Put on her new license plate

667. Make a collage of your best times.

668. Give him a key to your car.

669. Have a giant cookie baked that says "I love you" on it in icing.

670. Name your cute puppy after her.

671. Write love letters at least monthly.

---

*Only a life lived for others is a life worthwhile.*
—ALBERT EINSTEIN

---

672. Tell your lover's friends how you feel.

673. Write a book about your love.

674. Leave a love note in his car.

675. Do his laundry.

676. Serve breakfast in bed.

677. Plan and prepare a romantic five-course dinner.

678. Send flowers to the office.

679. Pick up his prescription when he is ill.

680. Buy him a can of Ralph Lauren tennis balls

681. Leave a love note hidden under the pillow.

682. Wear a T-shirt with her picture on it.

683. Let her join your fantasy sports league.

684. Pen a note in a romantic novel that the story is great, but your own love story is better.

685. Create shared goals.

686. Suffer through old home movies together.

687. Play his favorite childhood game some Saturday afternoon.

688. Find her lost pet.

689. Be a good sport while attending a high school reunion.

690. Express your feelings for her on your beach towel.

691. Put your feelings on a puzzle and send it through the mail.

692. Paint her a picture.

693. Shampoo her hair.

694. Send his mom flowers on his birthday as a "thank you" for having him.

695. Surprise him with a handsome desk set for his office.

696. Balance her checkbook.

697. Make him an Easter basket filled with his favorite candies.

698. Remember all of your anniversaries.

699. Tease lightly.

700. Have a special knock on the door that only the two of you know.

701. Guard against jealousy.

702. Videotape important moments in your relationship.

703. Read the great books on religion for the deeper meanings of love.

704. Bring her home-grown goodies from your garden.

705. Build her a dream doll house that will house her television set.

706. Fix the leaky toilet.

707. Iron his shirts.

708. Buy new shoe strings for his tennis shoes.

709. Pick up her mail when she is out of town.

710. Give him your picture for his desk at the office.

711. Add her name to your charge cards.

712. Listen to his troubles.

713. Sing "your song" together.

714. Plan and take a dream vacation to Paris (it is so romantic!).

715. Have a catered lunch picnic in his office.

716. Buy a house together.

717. Sleep on satin sheets.

718. Carve your initials on a tree.

719. Change her flat tire.

720. Send a loving message by carrier pigeon.

721. Cook a fabulous dinner for her when she needs a break from the kitchen.

722. Attend her office functions.

723. Stand close when talking.

**724.** Rent a cabin on a lake in the woods for a weekend.

**725.** Ask questions about his day.

**726.** Share a booth at a cozy restaurant.

**727.** Take her mom to lunch.

**728.** Encourage her to go after the promotion at work.

---

*Time is the most valuable thing a man can spend.*

—THEOPHRASTUS

---

**729.** Accompany her to the mall.

**730.** Surprise her by paying off her Visa bill.

**731.** Treat him to a new tie for his job interview.

**732.** Read "how to" books on how to have a healthy relationship.

**733.** Hire a maid for your not-so-tidy mate.

**734.** Encourage her to learn self-defense.

**735.** Spruce up her dull apartment with a fresh coat of paint.

**736.** Send a Valentine in January to get things rolling.

**737.** Learn to ask for forgiveness.

**738.** Be flexible.

**739.** Split expenses for a great evening out.

740. Refrain from trying to run her life.

741. Be willing to go the extra mile.

742. Take flowers to the graves of his loved ones.

743. Have a weekly relationship check up.

744. Tell everyone that you love him.

745. At a red light, get out of your car and publicly proclaim your love for her.

746. Give her a piggyback ride when she is tired of walking.

747. Accompany him to the doctor when he is really sick.

748. Encourage her to stop smoking.

749. Don't let him drink and drive.

750. Help each other make it through Friday the 13th.

751. Tell him that he is your hero.

752. Needlepoint a belt for him.

753. Put the top back on the toothpaste.

754. Open a charge account for her at a chic new boutique, with a credit balance already on it.

755. Engrave two mugs with your initials.

756. Hide favorite candies around the house

757. Telephone when you are out with the guys.

758. Be a big brother to her younger siblings.

759. Learn to speak French (it sounds so romantic).

**760.** Purchase a work of art that you first saw together.

**761.** Do his holiday shopping for him.

**762.** Monogram her handkerchiefs with your initials.

**763.** Rub Ben Gay on his sore muscles.

**764.** Hire a high school band to come and play "your song" at his house.

**765.** Buy him the winning lottery ticket.

**766.** Have a fireplace in your bedroom.

**767.** Rent a yacht for a dreamy evening.

**768.** Advertise your feelings in the yellow pages of your local telephone book.

**769.** Take him someplace where he has never been before.

**770.** Write your feelings for each other in the sand at the beach.

**771.** Live by the motto that actions speak louder than words.

**772.** Pay for her membership to a romance novel book club.

**773.** Share a sleeping bag made for two on a camping trip.

**774.** Declare your love in writing.

**775.** Spend the night in a feather bed.

*We should give as we would receive, cheerfully, quickly, and without hesitation, for there is no grace in a benefit that sticks to the fingers.*
　　　　　　　　　　　　　　　　—SENECA

776. Finish the jigsaw puzzle that he couldn't put together.

777. Share your Oreo cookies.

778. Give her a ride to and from the airport on her next business trip.

779. Buy extra copies of the newspaper anytime your loved one is in it.

780. Fix him a midnight snack.

781. Place your feelings in a bottle and set it sailing in the ocean.

782. Cultivate romance.

783. Put your loved one in your will.

784. Learn to be a good winner.

785. Look for the good in your love.

786. Make love in front of a roaring fire.

787. Reveal your secret wishes.

788. Cut his morning toast into a heart shape

789. Send only romantic holiday greeting cards.

790. Clean the snow off of his car after a big storm.

791. Delight yourselves in a long after-dinner talk.

**792.** Have your feelings printed on pencils.

**793.** When you are buying cosmetics, pick up a few aftershave samples for him.

**794.** Kidnap him from work when he has been working long hours.

**795.** Share your dreams.

**796.** Host a garage sale to get rid of her junk.

**797.** Scare him to cure him of the hiccups.

**798.** Give little forehead kisses.

**799.** Make a lover's knot when you need to tie something together.

**800.** Fetch the morning paper so that she can read it in bed.

**801.** Slip your own private message inside your partner's fortune cookie.

**802.** Go see a romantic tear-jerker instead of the latest blockbuster.

**803.** Drift away from your troubles on a raft together.

**804.** Build a snowman with a red heart.

**805.** When her budget says hamburger, treat her to steak.

**806.** Collaborate on a project together.

**807.** Tie the knot.

**808.** Warm the towels while your mate takes a shower.

**809.** Put a piece of chocolate on her pillow.

810. Gently wake him up when he is having a nightmare.

811. Give a copy of this book (after highlighting your personal favorites).

812. Be the first one to jump out of bed to turn off the alarm clock.

813. Help her to rearrange her furniture.

814. Grill a giant T-bone steak for two.

815. Share your blanket at a cold football game.

816. Have a heart-to-heart talk at midnight.

817. Sharpen all of his pencils.

818. Buy her a special pillowcase.

819. Treat each other as partners.

820. Collect souvenirs from your trips.

821. Find out what your lover thinks is sexy.

822. Sneak an afternoon nap together.

823. Rid yourselves of traditional gender-based roles.

824. Embroider matching chambray shirts.

825. Give great gifts that come in small packages.

826. Imagine that you are the only two people in the world.

827. Mark a calendar of memorable occasions from your relationship.

828. Send her travel brochures and let her choose your next vacation destination.

> *He who forgives ends the quarrel.*
> —AFRICAN PROVERB

829. Enjoy the specialness of setting up your first home together

830. Have a pillow that says "Tonight" on it (and put it to use often).

831. Celebrate with an anniversary cake that looks like your wedding cake.

832. Always say "good night."

833. Curl up side by side with good books

834. Pray for each other.

835. Stay together at parties.

836. Save the ticket stubs from all of your theater dates.

837. Plan for your future with a joint retirement account.

838. Team up to do household chores

839. Pop the big question.

840. Send a bouquet of balloons.

841. Learn the art of compromise.

842. Escape to Bermuda for a long weekend.

843. Set the alarm on a weeknight just to make love.

844. Spray your love letters with perfume.

845. Write a new stanza to a famous poem.

**846.** Call him your Prince Charming.

**847.** Put sun screen on his bald spot

**848.** Hide love notes in plastic Easter eggs

**849.** Hold hands while praying

**850.** File a joint tax return.

**851.** Proudly display your wedding invitation

**852.** Always have his favorite beverage on hand

**853.** Drift off to sleep in each other's arms.

**854.** Believe in miracles.

**855.** Monogram your towels with "His" and "Hers"

**856.** Find your own tropical paradise (create one with a sun lamp if you have to).

**857.** Be a source of inspiration for your partner.

**858.** Buy her a sexy black cocktail dress.

**859.** Give any heart-shaped gift.

**860.** Show pride in his childhood accomplishments.

**861.** Send his mom a casserole when she is under the weather.

**862.** Escort her to her wedding gown fittings.

**863.** Take his arm whenever you cross the street

**864.** Toast each other on every anniversary.

**865.** Put butter on her cooking burn.

**866.** Bring her a piping hot cup of coffee in the morning.

**867.** Save the last piece of pizza for him.

**868.** Play kissy face.

**869.** At a formal dinner, play footsies under the table.

**870.** Compose year-end holiday letters to his friends

---

*In this world, one must be a little too kind to be kind enough.*

—MARIVAUX

---

**871.** Dream of the fun times to come.

**872.** Fill a piñata with special, personal gifts.

**873.** Know how to eat humble pie without choking.

**874.** Have the piano player dedicate a special song.

**875.** Give each other goose bumps.

**876.** Brown nose his boss for him.

**877.** Put together a portfolio of your best times and place it in his briefcase.

**878.** Meet for a Victorian tea in a romantic country inn.

**879.** Loan her your cashmere sweater.

**880.** Wear his team jacket.

**881.** Never write a "Dear John" letter.

**882.** Lend him your favorite book.

**883.** Rent a summer house.

884. Lock your office door and take the time to say hello properly.

885. Reveal your secret fears.

886. Pull out her chair at the dinner table.

887. Watch the sun rise arm in arm.

888. Flirt for no particular reason.

889. Reassure him while he is waiting for test results to come back from the doctor.

890. Surrender before an argument becomes too lengthy.

891. Have a romantic picnic in a field of summer wildflowers.

892. Accept her collect phone calls.

893. Believe in the strength of your love.

894. Work at being uninhibited around each other.

895. Volunteer to help him do some awful household chore.

896. Give him your unlisted telephone number.

897. Have a suit custom tailored for him.

898. Hide a gift in the glove compartment.

899. Cheer the loudest at his game.

900. Share a park bench, but only use half of it so you can sit really close.

901. Treat him to homemade desserts for an entire month.

902. Even when you know what he is going to say before he says it, allow him to finish his sentence.

**903.** Make sure that the only name calling you do is something romantic.

---

*A good intention clothes itself with power.*
—RALPH WALDO EMERSON

---

**904.** Program his new computer for him.

**905.** Get excited about seeing each other again.

**906.** Wish that you had a twin bed instead of a queen so that you could snuggle more.

**907.** Share the same pillow all night.

**908.** Hold hands during religious services.

**909.** Write a note in glow-in-the-dark ink.

**910.** Wish him "sweet dreams" nightly.

**911.** Believe that you are the best couple that you know.

**912.** Laugh at the same things.

**913.** Dream of being millionaires together.

**914.** Be "in the mood."

**915.** Take a composition class so you can write better love letters.

**916.** Read "Blondie" together.

**917.** Spend Saturday night doing what your mate wants to do instead of always doing what you want to do.

**918.** Hunt for his lost possessions.

919. Buy him a box of Band-Aids when you have wounded his heart.

920. Make a gift instead of always buying one.

921. Stand in a long line to get her tickets to the show of her dreams.

922. Celebrate the fact that God brought you two together.

923. Dress up for dates.

924. Sew name tags in his clothes that go to the laundry.

925. Play tic tac toe using hearts of pink and red.

926. Whisper to each other while in a crowd.

927. Convey your feelings by giving a gift of a charming Mary Engelbreit poster.

928. Realize that real romance doesn't have to cost a penny.

929. Hide a great gift in a florist box and make her think that she is just getting flowers.

930. Write loving comments on his morning newspaper.

931. Make a pass at her in public.

932. Pick out a diamond ring together.

933. Put an aspirin in her flowers to make them last longer.

934. Have linen handkerchiefs monogrammed for him with the date of when you met.

935. Foster the reputation of a fabulous couple.

936. Share all aspects of your life.

937. Imagine that the birds are singing just for the two of you.

938. Give her an exquisite evening bag with tickets to a wonderful show inside.

939. While away a Sunday afternoon on a porch swing.

940. Give her your old fraternity pin.

941. Present her with a blue ribbon the next time she cooks a wonderful meal.

942. Plan on growing old together.

943. Be glad that you two got married.

944. Pretend to like shopping for her sake.

945. Use the same expressions as your mate.

946. Realize that you have found your prince in him.

947. Dance together at wedding receptions.

948. Give him a lift to work.

949. Announce your feelings over a public address system.

950. Steal her away from work for a mid-morning coffee break.

951. Buy her anything made of silk.

952. Help keep the calm during an emergency.

953. Whistle her favorite song while you are in the shower.

954. Sit through the extra innings of a ball game without complaining.

955. Wake him up with beautiful chamber music.

Modern Anniversary Gifts:
*First – Clocks*
*Fifth – Silverware*
*Tenth – Diamond jewelry*
*Fifteenth – Watches*
*Twentieth – Platinum*
*Twenty-fifth – Silver*
*Thirtieth – Diamond*
*Fortieth – Ruby*
*Fiftieth – Gold*

956. Purchase two goldfish and name them after the two of you.

957. Visit the English countryside together.

958. Dry the first flowers he gave to you.

959. Keep in mind that these are the good old days.

960. Bring her a small gift when you are away on a business trip.

961. Realize that your relationship is better than any on "The Young and the Restless."

962. Hide a small present that may not be found for weeks.

963. The next time that you get an extra large paycheck, try sharing it.

964. Give a dollar for his thoughts instead of a penny.

**965.** Love the number two and all that it represents.

**966.** Wear matching hats to a ball game.

**967.** Keep his love letters hidden in a secret drawer.

**968.** Prepare a bath for her after a long, hard day.

**969.** Surprise her with extravagant holiday decorations.

**970.** Make him homemade preserves.

**971.** Put only her name in your little black book.

**972.** Search out a piece of jewelry that has a romantic history attached to it.

**973.** Wait for her before you start anything.

**974.** Be able to wear your "comfy" clothes around each other.

**975.** Daydream of being stranded on a desert island and share the fantasy.

**976.** Decorate his office with silk plants.

**977.** Make a gift statement by giving her a Baccarat vase with a single red rose.

**978.** Dine by the light of an oil lamp.

**979.** Make a paper heart chain and write little love notes on each heart.

**980.** Give second chances.

**981.** Have catalogues mailed to her from her favorite stores with your pet name for her on the address label.

**982.** Frame an entire wall with the greeting cards he has sent you over the years.

**983.** Bake him an angel food cake just because you think he is an angel.

**984.** On cold winter nights, use an old fashioned bedwarmer to make it cozy.

**985.** Decorate his car with helium-filled balloons.

**986.** Call her at midnight just to wish her a happy new day.

**987.** Give him two season tickets to his favorite sporting event (the catch is that he has to take you along).

**988.** Dazzle her with a diamond tennis bracelet the next time you are on the court.

**989.** Blush when you look deeply into his eyes.

**990.** Tell her she looks pretty even when she is in her old clothes.

**991.** Bring her a tulip on the anniversary of the day you first met.

**992.** Disguise your voice while making a fun and flirty phone call.

**993.** Keep her glass and hors d'oeuvre plate filled at the next party.

**994.** Leave a loving message on his computer screen.

**995.** Order checks with both of your names on the account.

**996.** Give heart-shaped chocolates throughout the year.

**997.** Make his family feel at home in your home.

**998.** If he is going to be in California, prepare for him an earthquake preparedness kit.

**999.** Buy him a pair of theme boxers for all major holidays.

---

# How to Write a Great Thank You Note:
*Make it personal*
*Have it from your heart*
*Tell why you are grateful*
*Be appreciative*
*Express why you like the gift*
*Be affectionate*
*Promise to get together soon*
*Say something nice about the giver*
*Be sure to handwrite the note*

---

**1000.** Send her a poinsettia for the holidays.

**1001.** Collect seashells from your times together at the seashore.

**1002.** Baby-sit her siblings.

**1003.** Ask him to carve the turkey at your family's Thanksgiving dinner.

**1004.** Bake cookies from his favorite childhood recipes.

**1005.** Wear matching sweaters to a holiday party.

**1006.** Treat her like a princess.

**1007.** Give him plenty of quiet time to enjoy his morning newspaper.

**1008.** Mark his professional calendar with important romantic events.

**1009.** Give her a card on Boss's Day just for a little joke.

**1010.** Meet her for lunch at the mall on her big shopping day.

**1011.** Help her catch the bride's bouquet at the next wedding.

**1012.** Stick a tiny love note in his jelly donut some morning.

**1013.** Dim all the lights.

**1014.** Dance to music from an old victrolla or gramophone.

**1015.** Send her a cute set of flannel PJs to keep her warm when you aren't around.

**1016.** Have the florist deliver an elegant centerpiece prior to a dinner party.

**1017.** Be gracious to all the people that work for him.

**1018.** Give a "blank book" filled with your feelings.

**1019.** Invite her out via a tape recorded message.

**1020.** Plan an elaborate theme date.

**1021.** Acknowledge all gifts in a big way.

**1022.** Send her a beautiful pair of pumps the morning of your date to go dancing.

1023. Learn the Heimlich maneuver if he cooks often (just kidding).

1024. When your budget won't allow for the real thing, give her a piece of costume jewelry.

1025. Always open her car door.

1026. Walk on the outside of the sidewalk and let her have the inside.

1027. Learn her coworkers' names.

1028. Display his sports trophies.

1029. Have Casey Kasem dedicate a song on the top forty countdown.

1030. Let her cut in line in front of you.

1031. Show a genuine and sincere interest in her friends.

1032. Carry your mate's shoes when she goes barefoot.

---

*People are often lonely because they build walls instead of bridges.*

—ANONYMOUS

---

1033. Check out a thesaurus to find new words to express your love.

1034. Wear matching sweatsuits to the gym.

1035. Needlepoint an eyeglass case for him.

**1036.** Celebrate Thanksgiving in a city where there is lots of snow for an old-fashioned Currier & Ive's holiday.

**1037.** Visit all of the famous honeymoon cities.

**1038.** Have her paged just so you can tell her you care.

**1039.** Give him your full attention while he is talking.

**1040.** Rent or buy him a big screen television for the Super Bowl.

**1041.** Give her your grandmother's broach that she has always admired.

**1042.** Never give her a practical gift unless she asks for one.

**1043.** Honestly answer questions about your future together.

**1044.** Hire a baby-sitter so you two can have a night out on the town.

**1045.** Take him to the new restaurant that is getting the rave reviews.

**1046.** Decorate her bedroom via a Laura Ashley store.

**1047.** Fill colored bottles with bath beads for her.

**1048.** Write a love letter on homemade stationary.

**1049.** Kiss to the big New Year's Eve countdown.

**1050.** Fix a windowsill box on her bedroom window.

**1051.** Call her mom when she gets sick.

1052. Lift her up on your shoulders so she can get the best view.

1053. Provide plenty of room in your relationship.

1054. Order for her when you are dining out.

1055. Treat her to a bottle of perfume instead of cologne.

1056. Hold hands while waiting for the results of a pregnancy test.

1057. Make a road map of where you are in your relationship and make plans for where you would like to go.

1058. Pamper her by finding a Victorian style bathtub for the bathroom.

1059. When one of you has been a rat, ask for forgiveness with a ten-pound block of cheese.

1060. Frame travel posters of places you have been together.

1061. Keep each other company to avoid being scared on Halloween.

1062. Order an ice cream cake for his birthday and have it delivered to his office.

1063. Foster her glamorous image by giving her a peignoir set.

1064. Sleep in a four-poster canopy bed.

1065. Knit him a muffler.

1066. Play tennis just so that you can play at love together.

**1067.** The next time he is out grilling, hand him a personalized branding iron for his steaks.

**1068.** Pay for her braces.

**1069.** When he gets a promotion, order elegant business cards for him.

**1070.** Watch the local paper for upcoming events that he will enjoy.

**1071.** Take turns reading a book on loving relationships.

**1072.** Rent a condo at the beach for him when he needs a break from work.

**1073.** Buy a winter sweater for her dog.

**1074.** Have your dream home built by her favorite architect.

**1075.** Send him a subscription to *The Wall Street Journal*.

**1076.** Have a signal that will let your partner know that you are in the mood.

**1077.** Blow heart-shaped bubbles with your bubblegum.

**1078.** Fill her mail box with wildflowers.

**1079.** Take Polaroid pictures of the guests at her next bash.

**1080.** Find the sheet music for "your song" and have the composer autograph it.

**1081.** Embroider your relationship motto for the wall of his den.

**1082.** Give her a book of gift certificates to McDonalds.

**1083.** Create a homemade bookmark by laminating a poem or comic that has a special meaning.

**1084.** Have a book of beautiful stamps that are only used on love letters.

**1085.** Fill a basket with unique cookie cutters that represent a piece of your shared history.

**1086.** If he is always running late, help him out by giving him a handsome desk clock.

**1087.** Read a book about improving self-esteem (one can't love someone else without first being able to love him- or herself).

**1088.** Lip sync "your song" to her.

**1089.** Spend a weekend at a great ski resort in Aspen.

**1090.** Buy the drinks when he takes you out for dinner.

**1091.** Put toothpaste on his toothbrush and leave it by the sink for him to find in the morning.

**1092.** Send a friendship card.

**1093.** Release hundreds of balloons on his birthday.

**1094.** Treat him to a great haircut by a stylist instead of the corner barber.

**1095.** Test the battery in her car before the onset of winter.

**1096.** Make your next bicycle purchase a bicycle built for two.

> *A palace without affection is a poor hovel,*
> *and the meanest hut with love in it is a*
> *palace for the soul.*
> —ROBERT G. INGERSOLL

**1097.** Send him to the batting cages for a Saturday afternoon.

**1098.** Have the florist send her a get-well bouquet when she is sick.

**1099.** Design a badge that says she is the world's best lover.

**1100.** Give him an autograph from his childhood hero

**1101.** When he gets that new sports car, give him some stylish new hub caps.

**1102.** Have the bakery bake his birthday cake in the shape of his favorite sport.

**1103.** When you know that you hold the winning lottery ticket, give it to him.

**1104.** Install an air conditioner in her apartment.

**1105.** Buy him a vintage car from the year he was born for a milestone birthday.

**1106.** Advertise your feelings on public access stations.

**1107.** Send her flowers on the birthdays of your children.

**1108.** Treat her to a make over at a famous salon.

**1109.** Keep your television on ESPN for him.

**1110.** Make a money wreath for her during a hard luck holiday.

**1111.** Place your picture in her locket.

**1112.** Work to help save her favorite endangered species.

**1113.** For a great pick me up, treat her to a face lift.

**1114.** Surprise her by setting the table with holiday china.

**1115.** On a cold night, cuddle up under floral flannel sheets.

**1116.** Place a heart-shaped sucker on her plate after dinner for dessert.

**1117.** Do the unexpected.

**1118.** If your hotel room has two single beds, slide them together

**1119.** Hold each other.

**1120.** Place a sterling silver comb and brush set on her dressing table.

**1121.** For a wonderful surprise, purchase the famous his and her Neiman-Marcus gifts.

**1122.** Send a huge wedding cake to her office on your anniversary.

**1123.** Create a self-improvement agenda for your half of the relationship.

**1124.** When the car windows fog up, write both of your initials inside of a heart.

1125. Hand her a wand and a crown and treat her like a fairy princess on your evening out on the town.

1126. Play the game of twenty questions to get to know each other all over again.

1127. Stay home on New Year's Eve for a private celebration.

1128. March around the house arm in arm to the Wedding March.

1129. Give her a piggyback ride.

1130. Check her wrap for her when you go out for the evening.

1131. Know him well enough to be able to pick him out in his family's childhood photo albums.

1132. Screen her calls when she is home sick.

1133. Buy him a cellular phone so he can always take your call.

1134. Wrap his birthday gift in a box within a box and put a love letter inside.

1135. Record your feelings on a cassette tape and give it to your mate before you leave on a business trip.

1136. Polish his hardwood floor.

1137. Place a first aid kit in his boat.

1138. Have a paper doll made with her face on it.

1139. Pose for a romance novel–type photograph.

1140. Send flowers when she is out of town on business.

**1141.** Give the gift of a great shared memory.

**1142.** Bring her a cup of herbal tea when she is working late

---

Popular Romantic Nicknames:
*Angel*
*Honey*
*Baby*
*Darling*
*Sweetheart*
*Dearest*
*Princess*
*Lover*

---

**1143.** Order an entire new wardrobe for her from the latest mail order catalogues

**1144.** Donate to the American Heart Association in honor of your relationship.

**1145.** Install a two-person jacuzzi in your home.

**1146.** When you are going to be out of town, stock up on gourmet TV dinners for him.

**1147.** Give her a beautiful beaded sweater for New Year's Eve.

**1148.** Place a cookbook on his kitchen shelf.

**1149.** Read her favorite childhood story to her as she drifts off to sleep.

**1150.** Proudly show your friends her photograph

**1151.** Put a love note in acrylic to make a paperweight

**1152.** Hang a cute picture of the two of you on your refrigerator door.

**1153.** Enroll him in an adult education class that he has been wanting to take.

**1154.** If she is on her feet all day, treat her to a Clairol foot massage machine.

**1155.** Take a Longaberger basket full of potted plants to her home for a mid-summer pick me up.

**1156.** Send him a subscription to *Sports Illustrated*

**1157.** Study a current issue of *Travel and Leisure* to plan a great vacation.

**1158.** Take his temperature when he is sick.

**1159.** Hang a feather boa next to her nightie.

**1160.** Get him an answering machine for his car phone.

**1161.** On a milestone anniversary, give her a diamond anniversary ring.

**1162.** Make him divinity when he has been heavenly to you.

**1163.** Search through antique stores to find an antique quilt for bundling.

**1164.** Pat him on the back for a job well done.

**1165.** Leave a flower on her windshield.

**1166.** When she moves to a new home, give her an elegant book on interior design.

**1167.** Hire a harpist to play during a special dinner.

**1168.** Write a love note on a balloon with a felt-tip pen

**1169.** Throw an un-birthday party for him.

**1170.** Invite her childhood friends and their dolls to an old-fashioned tea party in her honor.

**1171.** Create an obstacle course in your living room that will lead to a wonderful surprise present.

**1172.** Dress up as his favorite childhood character and serve him breakfast in bed on his birthday.

**1173.** Make heart-shaped candy sculptures using gum drops and marshmallows.

**1174.** Have a throne chair for him on his birthday at the dinner table.

**1175.** Host a birthday party for her boss.

**1176.** Embroider his barbecue apron with "World's Best Chef."

**1177.** Take her on a teddy bear tour of England by calling: Keystone Traders, Specialty Tours, Ltd., 505 West Broad Street, Chesaning, MI 48616, 1-800-826-1300.

**1178.** Create a treasure hunt to find a very special gift.

**1179.** Sing "Happy Birthday" every year.

**1180.** Dance the tango.

**1181.** Take her camping and hide love notes all around the campsite.

---

*Gratitude is the fairest blossom which springs from the soul.*
—HOSEA BALLOU

---

**1182.** Kiss while waiting at a railroad stop.

**1183.** When you first see each other from a distance give a big enthusiastic wave.

**1184.** The next time he is having the guys over, fix a ton of munchies.

**1185.** Serve a meal consisting of all of his favorite fast foods.

**1186.** Tolerate quirks.

**1187.** Give a heart-shaped key ring.

**1188.** Make up slogans that describe your relationship.

**1189.** Hire a well-known interior designer to decorate his new place.

**1190.** Make sure he gets enough time with the guys.

**1191.** Stop on your way home from work and pick up her favorite flavor of ice cream from Baskin Robbins.

**1192.** Send a map with a lunch invitation to meet you for a special, out of the way meal.

**1193.** Have the florist make up a beautiful bow for her Teddy Bear.

**1194.** Call AT&T to install video telephones in your office and hers so that you can always be in close communication.

**1195.** Make big plans for the weekend.

**1196.** Fill her car with flowers.

**1197.** Spend the weekend in bed.

**1198.** Build a campfire in your own backyard to snuggle and fix s'mores.

**1199.** Invite her coworkers over for a surprise birthday breakfast.

**1200.** Give him a trophy for being the world's best lover.

**1201.** Plan a golf outing for him and a friend at a wonderful resort.

**1202.** Invite him to a Sadie Hawkins dance.

**1203.** Send a formal invitation the next time you ask her out.

**1204.** Chauffeur her to the mall during the busy holiday rush.

**1205.** Hire a mime to express your love.

**1206.** When you forget her birthday, throw a belated birthday bash.

**1207.** Host a roast for him.

**1208.** At your graduation, write a loving message on the top of your cap.

1209. After his next promotion, host a little get together for his closest associates.

1210. Crown him "King for a Night."

1211. Produce a video of her friends and family sharing their feelings about her.

1212. Cancel a meeting in order to spend some time together.

1213. Splurge on a fabulous gift.

1214. Celebrate her twenty-ninth birthday again and again.

1215. Hold hands while arguing.

1216. Make up after every fight.

1217. Bring her a hostess gift the next time she invites you over for a special dinner.

1218. Serve her birthday cake on a sterling silver cake stand.

1219. Fold a love note inside the dinner napkin.

1220. Make him the honorary cookie tester the next time you do your holiday baking.

1221. Host a weight watching party with low calorie nibbles after he has reached his desired weight.

1222. Slow dance in the dark.

1223. Give your mate a fine music box

1224. Lie side by side on the beach on matching beach towels.

1225. Decorate with paper hearts all over the house.

**1226.** Ask her mom to help you shop for a gift for her.

**1227.** Learn CPR and first aid so that you can always take care of him.

**1228.** Pick her for your team to compete at party games.

**1229.** Wear her favorite aftershave.

**1230.** Try to remember all of his good points when you are angry with him.

---

*Give what you have.*
*To someone it may be better than you dare to think*

—HENRY WADSWORTH
LONGFELLOW

---

**1231.** Ask his mom to teach you how to make his favorite dish.

**1232.** Plan the wedding of your dreams.

**1233.** Stay married

**1234.** Look through your parents' wedding pictures together.

**1235.** Watch all the classic holiday movies and share old memories.

**1236.** Ask to be her Valentine.

**1237.** Have a standing New Year's Eve date.

1238. Serve heart-shaped sandwiches and red fruit punch for supper.

1239. Prepare a champagne breakfast.

1240. Listen to your parents' stories of their courtship days together.

1241. Have the gardener trim her shrubs into a heart.

1242. Secretly plant bulbs in his yard to bloom in the spring.

1243. Fix her a full English tea on a dreary winter's afternoon.

1244. Shop for decorations together to begin your own holiday traditions.

1245. Entertain him with a "this is your life" party

1246. Remember the first song that the two of you ever danced to and find a recording of it so you can dance to it again.

1247. Send flowers the day before a milestone birthday.

1248. Hang banners and streamers on her car that say, "I love you."

1249. Practice kissing (practice makes perfect).

1250. Teach your parrot to speak your feelings of love.

1251. Help remodel her home.

1252. When he is doing yard work, hide bags of goodies for him to find throughout the yard.

1253. Celebrate your relationship.

**1254.** View a romantic movie and discuss how it relates to your relationship.

**1255.** Have a regular mid-week date night.

**1256.** Buy him a jersey of his favorite team.

**1257.** Play charades that reveal your true feelings for one another.

**1258.** Dress alike at your next family gathering.

**1259.** Persuade all of her friends to parade in front of her house with get-well signs the next time she is really ill.

**1260.** Have an indoor picnic in front of the television the next time he has an important game to watch.

**1261.** Take a walk on a starry winter night.

**1262.** Give a heart-shaped box of candy in August instead of waiting until February.

**1263.** Take photos of him playing a sport or working on his hobby and have the best ones framed.

**1264.** If he likes to fish or hunt, invite his buddies for an early morning breakfast before they depart.

**1265.** Help her make up her mind when she shops.

**1266.** Prepare a romantic picnic that includes wine, cheese, fruit, French bread, and classical music.

**1267.** Sing "For He's a Jolly Good Fellow" at his next birthday party.

Think in These Terms When You Think
of Your Next Time Together:
*Adventure*
*Amusement*
*Fun*
*Merriment*
*Daring*
*Gaiety*
*Diversion*
*Platinum*
*Festivity*
*Passion*

1268. If he has to stay in the hospital for tests, throw a very small and informal party at his bedside.

1269. Save the icing knife for him to lick.

1270. Give coupons to do "yucky" household chores.

1271. Start a gift (such as the beginning of a pearl necklace) that can be added to year after year and that lends to the promise of a future together.

1272. Learn the facts about AIDS prevention.

1273. Place a Cupid on his pillow on February 13th, to remind him of the big day.

1274. Hire a local seamstress to make a heart theme quilt for her.

1275. Get a celebrity to send her a birthday card or at least an autographed picture.

1276. Send her a May Day bouquet.

1277. Teach his dog to deliver your love letter.

1278. Give her a beautiful red dress on Valentine's Day.

1279. Place a box of heart-covered Band-Aids in her hiking boots.

1280. On July 4th, write your own couples' Declaration of Independence from ever being single again.

1281. Tie little love notes to his shrubs.

1282. Loose track of time when you are together

1283. When you set the dinner table, surprise her with heart-shaped place mats.

1284. Give a great foot message.

1285. Rent the movie *When Harry Met Sally*.

1286. Pay for his parking ticket.

1287. Take her to see a romantic play.

1288. Give him a tie with hearts on it.

1289. Hold hands while ice skating.

1290. Buy his dog a bone.

1291. Decorate the sack of her brown bag lunch with hearts.

1292. Take a late evening dinner dance cruise.

**1293.** Enter a contest together and share the prize.

**1294.** Invite your friends over for a slide show of the best times of your relationship.

**1295.** Speak in a romantic French accent for an entire date.

**1296.** Have your own private jokes

**1297.** Paint a mural that depicts special moments in your relationship.

**1298.** Play Scrabble using only romantic words

**1299.** Dress like her dream guy for at least one night out on the town.

**1300.** Give him a box of Dreamsicles since he is your dream guy.

**1301.** Arrange for a children's choir to serenade her

**1302.** Introduce your loved one to your family.

---

*Friendship is the only cement that will ever hold the world together.*

—WOODROW WILSON

---

**1303.** Write a critic's review of your relationship.

**1304.** Serve heart-shaped cookies with afternoon tea.

**1305.** Send Victorian style greeting cards.

**1306.** Give a first edition copy of a favorite book.

**1307.** Buy matching outfits in preparation for your romantic ski trip.

**1308.** Have dinner in front of a roaring fire.

**1309.** Create your own relationship trivia game.

**1310.** Decorate the front door with a welcome home sign for when he returns from a business trip.

**1311.** Instead of after dinner drinks, have after dinner gifts.

**1312.** Mark a globe with all the places to which you would like to travel together.

**1313.** Have your own film festival of your home videos of the two of you.

**1314.** Fly a welcome flag whenever she comes to visit.

**1315.** When traveling by car, stop at a roadside stand to buy your mate a flower.

**1316.** Buy her a mum corsage at the homecoming football game.

**1317.** Bake a fortune cake using charms and buttons that gives clues about the future of your relationship (be careful eating this one).

**1318.** Treat her to a romantic frock by designer Jessica McClintock.

**1319.** Answer mail from him promptly.

**1320.** Have a cheese tray waiting in his hotel room when he is away on business.

**1321.** Lend her your company's premises for her to have a party or meeting.

**1322.** Endow a chair in an educational field in her honor.

**1323.** Slip a $100 bill in her purse before she goes shopping.

**1324.** Poke around antique shops for gifts with romantic histories.

**1325.** Enlist the aid of a personal shopper at the best department store in town to help you pick out a birthday outfit for her.

**1326.** Check out museum shops for an unusual gift for his office.

**1327.** Raise your glass to her in a special salute at her next dinner party.

**1328.** Shoot him a "come hither" look.

**1329.** Make up fun and sexy innuendos.

**1330.** Send a bouquet of forget me nots.

**1331.** Share the same compartment while going through a revolving door.

**1332.** Honk at him when you see him on the street.

**1333.** Lay your coat across a puddle for her to walk over.

**1334.** Send flowers after a memorable date.

**1335.** Take a trip on the Orient Express.

**1336.** Leave a trail of flower petals so she can find you waiting for her.

**1337.** Have an exotic dinner flown in from a world class restaurant.

**1338.** Take a mini-vacation in your own town.

**1339.** Put your feelings on a billboard on the local bus.

**1340.** Send two dozen roses instead of one.

**1341.** Host a bon voyage party before his next trip.

**1342.** Hire a famous author to write the story of your relationship.

**1343.** Print your feelings on cocktail napkins.

**1344.** Send the queen of hearts playing card with a little love note written on it.

**1345.** Play the game of Scruples.

**1346.** Prepare a romance basket that includes candles, mood music, and perfume.

**1347.** Place an ad in her favorite magazine declaring your love for her.

**1348.** Tie red ribbons on her plants for Valentine's Day.

---

*Nothing great was ever achieved without enthusiasm.*
—RALPH WALDO EMERSON

---

**1349.** Have a favorite photograph of the two of you made into a life-sized poster.

**1350.** Exchange gifts on Saint Nicholas Night (December 6th).

**1351.** Send a bouquet of mistletoe.

**1352.** Find the time for a garden picnic on May Day.

**1353.** Relax side by side while sharing a hammock.

**1354.** Kiss whenever you walk through a doorway at the same time.

**1355.** Hug the first time you see each other each and every day.

**1356.** Practice some PDAs (Public Displays of Affection) to let the world know how you feel.

**1357.** Compliment his cooking.

**1358.** Seal a romantic moment with a kiss.

**1359.** Rake her leaves.

**1360.** Turn off the lights and share a prime spot next to the window to enjoy a late summer evening thunderstorm.

**1361.** Send an anniversary telegram.

**1362.** Exchange gifts on New Year's Day to get the year off to a great start.

**1363.** Buy a dual-controlled electric blanket

**1364.** Turn off the television set during mealtime.

**1365.** Make Saturday morning breakfast into a food extravaganza.

**1366.** Carry her briefcase home from work.

**1367.** Encourage her in her hobbies.

**1368.** Walk her dog on cold rainy nights.

**1369.** Kiss tenderly.

**1370.** Give her a gift certificate from Victoria's Secret.

1371. Request a fiftieth wedding anniversary card from the President of the United States. Make requests to White House Greetings Department, Executive Office Building 39, Washington DC 20500.

1372. Dance to her favorite music.

1373. Frame pictures of special times shared.

1374. Say "I love you" each and every time the urge hits you.

1375. Throw an "I'm glad you are in my life" party in his honor.

1376. Clean up his mess.

1377. Tell your mutual friends how much you care for each other.

1378. Hide a love note in his office.

1379. Mow his grass.

1380. Put a note in a brown bag lunch.

1381. Have joint mad money for a wild and crazy time out.

1382. Remember the exact moment that you fell in love.

1383. Write a poem about your love for each other.

1384. Rent a billboard to express your feelings for all of the world to see.

1385. Print your feelings on a kite and fly it.

1386. Write your feelings in icing on her birthday cake.

**1387.** Give a gift certificate from Crabtree and Evelyn.

**1388.** Take her often to her favorite restaurant.

**1389.** Go to counseling together to help get through a rough time.

**1390.** Invite her single friend along on your dates.

**1391.** Write a loving message on his baseball mitt.

**1392.** Help your mate recapture his childhood at Disneyland.

**1393.** Have your portraits made.

**1394.** Wear similar styles of clothing.

**1395.** Send his secretary a box of candy for putting up with all of your phone calls.

**1396.** Join the "mile high" club.

**1397.** Put up with his story telling when he's with his friends.

**1398.** Paint your bedroom passion pink.

**1399.** Throw a surprise party.

**1400.** Make a wreath for his front door.

**1401.** Write a fun little note on a dyed Easter egg.

**1402.** Send a provocative Valentine's Day card.

**1403.** Bring her chocolates and flowers on February 14th.

**1404.** Reminisce about old times spent together.

> *Good to forgive;*
> *Best to forget.*
> —ROBERT BROWNING

**1405.** Control your temper.

**1406.** Fix freshly squeezed orange juice or lemonade.

**1407.** Have your friends reinforce your feelings of love for your mate.

**1408.** Pick a bouquet of flowers for him from your garden.

**1409.** Send a sexy telegram.

**1410.** Buy her a puppy from one of the Westminster Dog Show winners.

**1411.** Pack his clothes for his next business trip.

**1412.** Save the newspapers when he is out of town for him to read when he returns.

**1413.** Stand up for your mate when the rest of the world seems to be dumping on him.

**1414.** Treat each other like royalty by staying in an English manor house.

**1415.** Pick out fun activities for future times together while reading *2002 Things to Do on a Date*.

**1416.** Record your feelings on a piece of paper and place it inside a balloon and set it free.

**1417.** If she is new in town, prepare her a directory of local hot spots.

**1418.** Buy a copy of your mate's favorite childhood book.

**1419.** Ask each other for advice.

**1420.** Always speak kindly.

**1421.** Praise him in front of his boss.

**1422.** Wallpaper her apartment.

**1423.** Learn not to hold grudges.

**1424.** On a busy day, screen his calls so that he can play catch up.

**1425.** Dine out often.

**1426.** Go to a tacky honeymoon resort and do all of the typical newlywed activities.

**1427.** Find a song that expresses your feelings.

**1428.** Encourage him to call his mother regularly.

**1429.** Be faithful.

**1430.** Bake his dad a cake or some cookies.

**1431.** Limit the red meat in his diet.

**1432.** Make love outside during a summer thunderstorm.

**1433.** Be a good sport and share any available space in your suitcase.

**1434.** Make the next Valentine's Day memorable by sending a dozen cards instead of just one.

**1435.** Chop firewood for her in preparation for a cold winter's night.

**1436.** Constantly work on improving your relationship.

**1437.** Refrain from trying to change your mate.

**1438.** Make your shoulder available during hard times so that she may lean on it

**1439.** Pretend to be great lovers like Mark Antony and Cleopatra.

**1440.** Say grace together.

**1441.** Remain open to new ideas.

**1442.** Acknowledge your mistakes readily.

**1443.** Be willing to share your successes.

**1444.** Order room service for a fabulous breakfast

**1445.** Start a collection of menus from your favorite restaurants and learn to cook his favorite dishes.

**1446.** Slow dance closely.

**1447.** Tear up your love letters from all old loves.

---

*Love does not dominate; it cultivates.*
—JOHANN WOLFGANG VAN GOETHE

---

**1448.** Send one rose for each year that you have been together.

**1449.** Help her move to her new place.

**1450.** Ask a street musician to play "your song."

**1451.** Engrave your feelings on a fine pen.

**1452.** Bake homemade bread

**1453.** Take his car in for a tune up

**1454.** Baby him when he is under the weather

**1455.** Help her study for her driving test

**1456.** Make a list of her good qualities and present it to her.

**1457.** Commit her telephone number and address to memory.

**1458.** Shout your feelings into a cave and listen together to the echoes.

**1459.** Chisel your names on a rock formation.

**1460.** Treat her as if she has an hour glass figure when you are buying her lingerie.

**1461.** Rendezvous at a grand hotel for the afternoon.

**1462.** Wax her car.

**1463.** Have a candlelight dinner under the stars

**1464.** Hide a love note in a tiny gift-wrapped Limoge box.

**1465.** Play a romantic hit on a jukebox.

**1466.** Take tons of photographs of each other.

**1467.** To avoid sunburn, put suntan lotion on her.

**1468.** State your feelings at a news conference.

**1469.** Hire a magician to deliver one of your love letters in an unforgettable manner.

**1470.** Place a private message in a newsletter to which he subscribes.

**1471.** Take a stroll down a country lane in the fall.

**1472.** Make New Year's Eve resolutions to improve your relationship.

**1473.** Rent the triple Oscar winning romance *Casablanca*

**1474.** Take her to the symphony to enjoy romantic music.

**1475.** Share a two-straw soda.

**1476.** Nuzzle early and nuzzle often.

**1477.** Design a crossword puzzle containing your sentiments toward your loved one.

**1478.** In a pinch, hem his trousers.

**1479.** Bring him milk and cookies when he is working late.

**1480.** Express your affections in a message in freshly fallen snow.

**1481.** Take her to a restaurant with strolling musicians and request a love song.

**1482.** Be tenderhearted.

**1483.** When talking on the phone to each other, do not take other calls.

**1484.** After a shower, help her write thank you notes.

**1485.** Close all the curtains and play a game of strip poker.

**1486.** Share the intricacies of your day during conversation at dinner.

1487. Give her an old sweatshirt of yours to wear on a lazy Saturday.

1488. Count your joint blessings.

1489. Make her feel like she is your first love.

1490. Tear up all your photos from previous romantic relationships.

1491. Share your umbrella during a sudden downpour.

---

*When God measures a man, He puts the tape around the heart instead of the head.*
—ANONYMOUS

---

1492. Write a love note in the mud on a rainy day.

1493. Believe in the best of your mate.

1494. Cheat on your diets together.

1495. Take notice and appreciate all of the things your mate does for you.

1496. Help him solve the Sunday crossword puzzle.

1497. Make a wish list so she can get you what you want for your next birthday.

1498. Help him watch his cholesterol intake.

1499. Promise your love for all time.

1500. Cheer her up when she doesn't get the promotion.

1501. Do something nice for her that she will never know you did.

**1502.** Get tickets to a sold-out event that she desperately wants to attend.

**1503.** Push her in a swing.

**1504.** Be the first to wish her "Happy Birthday."

**1505.** Buy matching silk PJs.

**1506.** Give loads of TLC.

**1507.** Share your problems.

**1508.** Tickle her fancy.

**1509.** Gift wrap yourself in a huge box to be delivered.

**1510.** Talk mushy.

**1511.** Give her a Steiff teddy bear.

**1512.** Clip articles from magazines that will be of interest to him.

**1513.** Create a joint wish list.

**1514.** Return to the place where you first fell in love.

**1515.** Plan a holiday that would make Currier and Ives jealous.

**1516.** Get married all over again (to each other).

**1517.** Give up the urge to say, "I told you so."

**1518.** Hide candy hearts all over the house.

**1519.** Buy a book embosser that has both of your names on it.

**1520.** Arrange to have church bells play "your song" while you express your feelings.

1521. Mix up your own love potion with your old chemistry set.

1522. Say "God bless you" after she sneezes.

1523. Call her from the airport just to say goodbye again.

1524. Give the red carpet treatment for no special occasion.

1525. Make up a few words so you can have your own special vocabulary.

1526. Look through the eyes of love, even when you don't feel like it.

1527. Create a happy home environment.

1528. Carve a jack o'lantern with a heart on it.

1529. Buy her birthday present weeks before her big day.

1530. Sing a duet at a karaoke club

1531. Read his favorite book.

1532. Share the same philosophy about life

1533. Find something else to do while he returns to his childhood watching "The Three Stooges "

1534. Celebrate the red letter days in your relationship.

1535. Read your old love letters to each other.

1536. Send a gift from a mail order company.

1537. Spend an evening soaking in the hot tub.

1538. Pick out a fine china pattern.

1539. Create a homemade greeting card.

**1540.** Spend an evening together at home without the television.

**1541.** House sit his apartment while he is out of town.

**1542.** Call after your big presentation to let him know how you did on it.

**1543.** Always send a postcard when you are away on business.

**1544.** Give each other a graduation gift when your relationship reaches a new stage.

**1545.** Allow him to read your diary.

**1546.** Doodle your lover's name.

**1547.** Be totally at ease while sharing quiet times.

**1548.** Escape for a clandestine meeting at a bed and breakfast.

**1549.** Bring him a doggie bag with his favorite dessert.

**1550.** Look the other way when he does one of your pet peeves.

**1551.** Hide a love note in his pocket.

**1552.** Help him study for an exam

**1553.** Cherish the fact that you have someone special in your life.

**1554.** Let him sleep late while you do the Saturday chores.

**1555.** Sing together during religious ceremonies even if he can't carry a tune

*There is nothing in all the world like friendship, when it is deep and real.*
—THOMAS DAVIDSON

**1556.** Clip coupons to help stretch the family budget.

**1557.** Rent a video of one of the all-time great love stories, *Roman Holiday*.

**1558.** Cut out comic strips that relate to your relationship.

**1559.** Needlepoint covers for his golf clubs.

**1560.** Help her color her hair.

**1561.** Fall head over heels in love with each other again.

**1562.** Wash her hair in the falling rain.

**1563.** Make a funny comeback to his grumpy morning wisecrack.

**1564.** Be supportive in the delivery room during the birth of your child.

**1565.** Keep the cookie jar filled with his favorite cookies.

**1566.** Pretend not to notice his enlarging bald spot

**1567.** Always be on the lookout for a great gift for your lover.

**1568.** Help him win the contest at work.

**1569.** Have a Halcyon box made with your sentiment painted on the lid.

**1570.** Spend the night in a luxurious hotel suite.

**1571.** Splurge on a camel hair coat for him.

**1572.** Take an extended vacation just so you two can spend more time alone.

**1573.** Collapse in bed together after a long tiring day.

**1574.** Gaze at each other from across the room at a crowded party.

**1575.** Celebrate the longest night of the year in bed.

**1576.** Answer "yes" to the big question.

**1577.** If he loves winter, freeze snowballs for a mid-summer snowball fight.

**1578.** Meet for your own power lunch to negotiate your relationship contract.

**1579.** Have your baby bracelets framed together.

**1580.** Lie in bed listening to raindrops on your roof.

**1581.** Don't notice her dark roots.

**1582.** Crochet an afghan to keep him warm when you aren't around to do so.

**1583.** Darn his favorite jeans so that he will never have to throw them away.

**1584.** Return again and again to your honeymoon hotel.

**1585.** Invite your mate to listen to Barbra Streisand CDs.

**1586.** When you can't kiss him because of your cold, hand him a bag of Hershey Kisses as a substitute.

**1587.** Keep a piece of your wedding cake frozen forever.

**1588.** Take a late night cruise.

**1589.** Hide his clothes while he is showering for a good-humored little joke.

**1590.** Give her your seat on the subway.

**1591.** Make a joint wish on a shooting star.

**1592.** Purchase coordinating outfits for the next party that you will host together.

**1593.** Surprise him with a case of his favorite liqueur.

**1594.** Find the perfect antique roll-top desk for his den.

**1595.** Stop the elevator between floors to kiss.

---

Reasons People Marry:
*They fall in love*
*To have children*
*For companionship*
*It is the adult thing to do*
*For financial security*
*All their friends are married*

---

**1596.** Have a toll booth in your home where you must kiss to pass through.

**1597.** Love all of the gifts that he gives you.

**1598.** Be agreeable with each other over the morning newspaper editorials.

**1599.** Cohost a story hour to read to your children

**1600.** Never take your relationship for granted.

**1601.** Always have your toes touching in bed at night.

**1602.** Live by the motto that the best is yet to come, even if things are fabulous between you now.

**1603.** Have two phone lines so you can sit side by side and talk to your friends and still be together.

**1604.** Make copies of your best love letters and hide them all around the house

**1605.** Form your own two-person support group.

**1606.** Give diamond jewelry for no special occasion.

**1607.** Be apologetic when you find yourself in the doghouse to shorten your stay.

**1608.** Write love notes in his notebook.

**1609.** Gently pull out his first gray hair.

**1610.** Keep feeding nickels to the fortune and weight machine until it predicts something wonderful for your relationship.

**1611.** Make private time for just the two of you.

**1612.** Have knees that quiver when you kiss.

**1613.** Buy matching sleep masks for your eyes for when you are both feeling overly tired and rundown.

**1614.** Organize all of your old trip photos into an album.

**1615.** Place your picture in a fine leather frame on his desk.

**1616.** Give her your life preserver when the ship is sinking.

**1617.** Put your out of season attire in storage to create more closet space for her clothes.

**1618.** Teach him the words to all of your favorite songs so that you can sing together on your next long car trip.

**1619.** Give him the last drops of water from your canteen while you are sightseeing in the desert

**1620.** Put a "Gone Fishing" sign on your office door and make love the rest of the afternoon

**1621.** Relive the romance of *To Catch a Thief*.

**1622.** Frame the most romantic cards that you have ever sent to each other.

**1623.** Listen to his grandparents tell stories of his childhood.

**1624.** Give her your jacket to stay warm.

**1625.** Gladly eat the burned piece of toast.

**1626.** Be a good sport when your mate pushes the snooze button three times before finally getting out of bed.

**1627.** Take lots of romantic holidays.

**1628.** Get up early and bring back breakfast from the best bakery in town while he sleeps.

1629. Keep a close eye on the mailbox for his love letters when he is out of town.

1630. Allow him to make his point even when you know he is wrong.

1631. Pass love notes during a meeting.

1632. Encourage him to reach his highest potential

1633. Improve his self-esteem by listing all of his achievements.

1634. Try to see eye to eye on important issues.

1635. Be frugal all year so that you can buy her a dream gift.

1636. Save his autograph from the first card that he sent to you as if it were a valuable treasure.

1637. Buy his favorite flavor of ice cream instead of yours.

1638. Bring her home flowers from the grocery when you do the marketing.

1639. Work at having "accidental" meetings so that you can see each other more often.

1640. Write a love letter together.

1641. Be nostalgic about your past together.

1642. Gladly give up your maiden name to take his name.

1643. Send her a Mother's Day card if she is a mom.

1644. Write Mrs. So-and-So over and over when you first fall in love to see how you would like having his name.

**1645.** Set a romantic table for breakfast.

**1646.** Invite him to your parents' home for Sunday dinners.

**1647.** Create events to look forward to.

**1648.** Throw a party for him when he is acting like a big baby and call it a baby shower (your friends will love it).

**1649.** Allow her to sample your meal while eating in a fine restaurant.

**1650.** If you don't like to go camping, go on an overnight picnic.

**1651.** Leave bad fights to the cats and dogs.

**1652.** When you are shopping together, sneak away to buy her a little surprise gift.

**1653.** Save your new outfit to wear with him.

**1654.** Reminisce about your wedding night.

**1655.** Unconsciously hum the same tune.

**1656.** Carry a rabbit's foot for his sake.

**1657.** In order to always be on time for your dates, give each other matching Rolex watches.

**1658.** Find an obscure address or book that your mate needs.

**1659.** Place cute stickers on your love notes.

**1660.** Check out a library book for him that you know he will enjoy.

**1661.** Give her a copy of a bridal magazine with a note telling her that she will always be your bride.

**1662.** Buy her a fun hat for her bad hair days.

**1663.** Take the long route to work just so you can spend more time together.

**1664.** Light up her life by giving her tons of candles.

**1665.** Hide a note in a book that you know she will buy at the bookstore.

**1666.** Enjoy having someone to split two-for-one sales with.

**1667.** Pack his brown bag lunch with gourmet food.

**1668.** When you use paper plates for supper, write a little love note around the border.

---

Reasons Why the Holidays Are Better if
You Are a Couple:
*Your lover can spoil you.*
*You can spoil your lover.*
*You can share holiday yummies in bed.*
*You can celebrate all night long.*

---

**1669.** Take her side when she has an argument with her girlfriend.

**1670.** Rent a flashing sign for the yard with a romantic message on it.

**1671.** Help his parents when they move to a retirement home.

1672. Keep her informed about what is happening when she has her eyes closed at a horror movie.

1673. Flatter him by making him think that you are jealous of his old girlfriend, even when you aren't.

1674. Share your first impressions of each other.

1675. Make a compliment list of all the nice things you have heard people say about her.

1676. Save some of his favorite old clothes for his son.

1677. Remind her to lock her car doors when she is out late at night without you.

1678. Speak highly of each other to your friends.

1679. Dream of your little boy growing up to be just like him.

1680. Dream of your little girl growing up to be just like her.

1681. Picture the two of you in the next Taster's Choice commercial.

1682. Send her her favorite flowers even when they are out of season.

1683. Drop out of the fast track so that you can spend more time with each other.

1684. View a foreign film and read only the romantic subtitles to each other.

1685. Think of him as TPOTL (The Pick of the Litter).

1686. Primp before you go out with him.

**1687.** Enjoy a harvest moon together.

**1688.** Buy unisex clothing to trade with each other.

**1689.** Always be on the lookout for romantic restaurants.

**1690.** Place sachets in her drawers.

**1691.** Treat her to a very expensive pair of leather gloves to keep her ring finger warm.

**1692.** Set a date for your wedding.

**1693.** Place a bouquet of flowers in every room of the house.

**1694.** Give her a lace hankie on the way to see a sad movie.

**1695.** Play show and tell with him after you spend the day at the mall.

**1696.** Renew your vows in a flashy Las Vegas ceremony.

**1697.** End all of your requests with the word "please."

**1698.** Try to fall asleep to dream the same dream.

**1699.** Say "we" instead of "I."

**1700.** Dial his number when you know he isn't home just to hear his voice on the answering machine

**1701.** Read her weight for her when she steps on the bathroom scale but is too afraid to look.

**1702.** If she loves Hollywood gossip, give her a subscription to *People* magazine

**1703.** Force him to eat healthy, cancer-fighting foods.

**1704.** Go for your premarital blood tests together.

**1705.** Smooch while sitting on the last row of seats on airplanes, buses, and trains.

**1706.** Take an apple to her teacher.

**1707.** Surprise her with the latest high fashion garment of the season.

**1708.** Kick the tires on her new car to check for possible problems.

**1709.** Rent all of the movies that her favorite star is in.

**1710.** Leave a message on the bathroom mirror with lipstick.

**1711.** Enter her in a contest for being the world's best mate.

**1712.** Support equality of the sexes.

**1713.** When she is upset after receiving a bad haircut, surprise her with a great looking wig.

**1714.** Buy him a diamond for a change.

**1715.** Share your roll of Lifesavers.

**1716.** Give her a red satin nightie.

**1717.** Write an inscription in each other's high school yearbook.

**1718.** Fill her makeup case with tubes of lipsticks in every color.

1719. Eat a string of licorice with each of you starting at opposite ends and working your way to the middle.

1720. Fill her closet with seven different pairs of Keds (one for each day of the week).

1721. Rent him a convertible for a summer weekend.

1722. Trim her bangs.

1723. Keep him up to date on men's fashion.

1724. Bring her a Spiegel catalog when she has been too busy to go shopping.

1725. Send him a news bulletin announcing your feelings regarding your relationship.

1726. Share a case of spring fever.

1727. Sign up to travel to the moon together.

1728. When he is home sick, bring him an armful of movies to keep him entertained.

1729. Be each other's best friends.

1730. The next time she buys a dress, surprise her with fabulous accessories for it.

1731. Give up your stereotypical beliefs about each other.

1732. Fix up his den to resemble the local gym with new weight lifting equipment.

1733. Send her a case of her favorite beauty product.

1734. If she loved Barbie Dolls as a child, find her the highly collectable Benetton model.

1735. Create a scrapbook at the end of the year of all of your best times together.

1736. Arrange to have a twenty-one gun salute done in his honor on a big birthday.

1737. Tuck love notes inside decorations when you pack them away to be found at the beginning of the next holiday season.

1738. Give her an AAA membership if she is on the road a lot.

1739. Say good night while your evening is still going fabulously.

1740. Forgive and forget.

1741. Write in calligraphy your loving thoughts.

1742. Send her flowers after she has a fight with her mom.

1743. Have an affair, but only with your spouse.

1744. Write your feelings on a paper airplane and sail it to her.

1745. Inquire about her plans for your future.

1746. Look for serendipitous experiences in your shared history.

1747. Give a gift for each little holiday throughout the year.

1748. Plan to visit Niagara Falls, the old honeymoon capital of the world.

1749. Act like you are a couple, instead of two single people.

> *We like someone because,*
> *We love someone although.*
> —HENRI DE MONTHERLANT

**1750.** Dry flowers from every bouquet that he sends to you

**1751.** Plant an herb garden for her.

**1752.** Send him a subscription to *Baseball Weekly* if he is a sports nut.

**1753.** Pick out your silver pattern.

**1754.** If she jogs, loan her your dog for safety.

**1755.** Give video rental certificates that can only be redeemed for times the two of you are together.

**1756.** Give him a copy of the latest "how to" book on his current household project.

**1757.** If he is a commuter, give him a roll of correct change.

**1758.** Make a cassette of all your favorite love songs.

**1759.** Treat her to a cosmetic bag filled with all kinds of expensive lotions and potions.

**1760.** Fill a small jewelry box with several pieces of gold jewelry.

**1761.** On Grammy Award night, pick out your new "love song" for the year.

1762. Make an evening of a progressive dinner at all of your favorite restaurants.

1763. Attend an event where formal attire is required.

1764. Let his dog sleep at the foot of the bed.

1765. Send her a lunch bouquet at work.

1766. Create an ad campaign about why she should love you

1767. Have your travel agent plan a surprise getaway for both of you.

1768. Stop for shopping breaks for her on your next vacation

1769. Borrow a friend's house for the night for an inexpensive getaway.

1770. Give her gift certificates for beauty treatments at the best salon in town.

1771. Stay home occasionally instead of going out with the guys.

1772. Throw a festschrift (where friends write tributes for the guest of honor).

1773. Pay for a hair transplant for his fiftieth birthday.

1774. Dress up like Rhett and Scarlet at your next Halloween party.

1775. Keep track of all of his relatives' birthdays and anniversaries.

1776. Give her a copy of Danielle Steel's most romantic book.

**1777.** Put on a puppet show that expresses your love.

**1778.** Call him right before his big meeting to wish him good luck.

**1779.** Make a crown for the birthday girl to wear during dinner.

**1780.** Spend the day on a farm getting close to nature and each other.

**1781.** Have a heart-to-heart pow-wow while sitting cross-legged on the living room rug.

**1782.** Write your feelings on the bottom of the pool (using indelible ink).

**1783.** Throw an old-fashioned slumber party on her birthday and invite all her old high school friends.

**1784.** Surprise her with a spring bonnet.

**1785.** Create a path from the front door to a special dinner location in your home.

**1786.** Dress up in your old college formal clothes and have your own nostalgic dance for two.

**1787.** When she has been acting crazy, send her a can of nuts with a funny little note tucked inside to break the tension.

**1788.** Reserve the bridal suite on your anniversary for the next thirty years.

**1789.** Create an old-fashioned "Most Wanted" poster with his picture on it.

**1790.** Make sure she votes.

1791. Create your own soap opera by filming the two of you in your own version of "General Hospital."

1792. Delay running the vacuum cleaner for two minutes during the running of the Kentucky Derby.

1793. When he runs in a marathon, provide him with drinks along the way.

1794. Tell only good humored jokes about your relationship.

1795. Give him a "Man of the Year" award and mark the occasion with the year in pictures.

1796. While sorting the mail, write love notes on the outside of the envelopes that don't belong to you.

1797. Rent for her the prime parking spot near her office.

1798. On her next birthday, throw a party in her honor at a local children's home.

1799. Hold her when she cries.

1800. Host a party for all of his brothers and sisters.

1801. Give him your own mini course on social graces.

1802. Set the dinner table as if you were entertaining the rich and famous when you have him over for dinner.

1803. Present her with a copy of the best-selling romance novel with the steamiest part of the book being your inscription.

---

Five of the Best Things to Say:
*I'm sorry*
*Thank you*
*Well done*
*You were right*
*Tell me about you*

---

**1804.** Fill his tool box with love notes.

**1805.** Install a lock on your bedroom door, if you have children.

**1806.** If he is new to the neighborhood, throw a party for all of his neighbors.

**1807.** Wait for him at the finish line no matter how long it takes for him to finish the race.

**1808.** Surprise his mom with a collage of his baby pictures.

**1809.** Serve heart-shaped cheese and crackers for a snack.

**1810.** Be kind to each other's parents.

**1811.** Plan a honeymoon evening where you decorate your house with posters of your honeymoon city and hotel.

**1812.** Go to a fine art gallery and purchase a work of art together.

**1813.** When you make a chef salad, cut the meat and cheese into heart shapes.

**1814.** Have your wedding pictures taken all over again on your tenth anniversary wearing your wedding attire.

**1815.** Rekindle the magic of when you first fell in love.

**1816.** Throw a reunion party for him with all of his friends from his old little league team.

**1817.** Teach her how to program the VCR.

**1818.** Bring along hot chocolate and cookies on a sleigh ride.

**1819.** Spend an evening writing joint letters to family and friends.

**1820.** Have the corner deli make box lunches for your date at the zoo.

**1821.** Serve breakfast on the patio.

**1822.** When he is going back for a college weekend with his friends, fix a tailgate party for them.

**1823.** Ask his buddies to send him a card when he down in the dumps and needs to know that he has people on his side.

---

*It is the most beautiful compensation of this life that no man can sincerely try to help another without helping himself.*
—RALPH WALDO EMERSON

---

**1824.** Barter together as a team with a vendor at a flea market.

1825. Ask your parents for their best advice on love and then share it.

1826. Give him box seats to the home opener.

1827. Hire a photographer to capture your date in pictures.

1828. Ask your friends to write their favorite memories of you as a couple for your next anniversary celebration.

1829. Give a copy of Eric Segal's *Love Story*.

1830. Spend an evening dancing to seductive Arabic music.

1831. Send silk roses instead of the real thing.

1832. Give him a red tie for Valentine's Day.

1833. Bake him a cherry pie to celebrate George Washington's birthday.

1834. Prior to his next trip, arrange for his friends to meet for a farewell party in the airport lounge.

1835. Have your silhouettes made together by a paper artist.

1836. Write a romantic limerick.

1837. On Saint Patrick's Day, write love notes on green shamrocks.

1838. Write a love note backwards for her to decipher in the bathroom mirror.

1839. Share your wishes of what your relationship will be in five, ten, and twenty years.

1840. Give little, fun gag gifts.

1841. Rent a party boat for just the two of you to enjoy a late night cruise.

1842. Send a huge box of children's valentines to her at work.

1843. When things are moving too fast, send a homemade speeding ticket.

1844. Give her a Raggedy Ann doll because she is the only doll that has a heart.

1845. Place heart-shaped doilies under the cookies you serve.

1846. Take her to a candy store and buy her every single piece of heart-shaped candy in the store.

1847. Try saying a loving thought in Pig Latin.

1848. Send him a red rose boutonniere.

1849. Take him to see his favorite sports hero.

1850. Make a special occasion out of all of your firsts as a couple.

1851. Have shirts custom made for him.

1852. Ask the DJ at the local dance club to dedicate a song to her.

1853. Hire a band to play at your home when it is just the two of you.

1854. Rent the movie theater to show her all-time favorite film.

1855. In order not to awaken your mate, read your book under the covers with a flashlight.

1856. Smooch.

**1857.** Use soft lighting.

**1858.** Have an in-home progressive dinner where each course is served in a different room.

**1859.** Play "Name that Tune" for all of the songs that have been meaningful in your courtship.

**1860.** Plan a surprise date for the weekend and give hints all week long to add to the fun and excitement leading up to the date.

**1861.** Have a gender exchange night where you switch roles in your relationship.

**1862.** Find a mascot that stands for your relationship.

**1863.** Host your own private slumber party for two.

**1864.** Float heart-shaped ice cubes in his drink.

---

*To love anyone is nothing else than to wish that person good.*
—THOMAS AQUINAS

---

**1865.** Give him an ornament that says he is the world's best. . . .

**1866.** Sneak his favorite food into the movies.

**1867.** Bring ice cream when your mate has a sore throat.

**1868.** Leave work problems at the office.

**1869.** Play two-handed solitaire.

1870. Check with your partner before accepting an invitation that involves both of you.

1871. Place a Valentine's Day classified ad.

1872. Check on things that go bump in the night for her sake.

1873. Dust the high places that she can't reach.

1874. Buy a "You Are Special Today" plate and use it throughout the year.

1875. Celebrate your differences.

1876. Splurge on a great bottle of wine and save it for your twenty-fifth wedding anniversary.

1877. Be a sport and ski with her on the bunny slope.

1878. Plan a rendezvous in the bathroom while at a party.

1879. Be a little unpredictable.

1880. Loan her your razor in a pinch.

1881. Give only low calorie candy when she is on a diet.

1882. Check with him before pitching his old magazines.

1883. When your mate has locked himself out of the house, let him back in.

1884. Share your inheritance.

1885. Gladly wear the ugly sweater she gave you.

1886. Celebrate a big birthday for an entire month with a cake countdown (one cake delivered each week).

**1887.** On her birthday give her a present at breakfast, lunch, and dinner.

**1888.** Buy all kind of party favors for her next birthday celebration.

**1889.** Write a personal letter of congratulations whenever she gets a promotion at work.

**1890.** Introduce your mate proudly when you run into your friends.

**1891.** Prepare his favorite casserole dish in advance when you can't be home to fix dinner.

**1892.** Answer your phone in a friendly and warm manner when you are expecting a call from her.

**1893.** Recommend her to your boss for a position within your company when she is in the job market.

**1894.** Show a genuine interest in what he has to say.

**1895.** Support her fund-raising efforts for her pet organization.

**1896.** Place an ad expressing your love in a program of an event that you plan to attend together.

**1897.** Design a discreet ad to run in his professional journal that tells of your love.

**1898.** Give a grant in his name for research in an area that has special meaning to him.

**1899.** Host a fund-raising dinner to benefit her favorite charity.

1900. Have someone with impeccable taste pick out your gifts for her.

1901. Collect souvenirs of your fun times together for an entire year.

1902. Donate a piece of medical equipment to a local hospital in her honor.

1903. If your company gives away promotional items, save one for him.

1904. Splurge on a fabulous weekend at The Plaza Hotel in New York City.

---

*Love does not consist in gazing at each other, but in looking together in the same direction.*
—ANTOINE DE SAINT-EXUPÉRY

---

1905. Whistle at her when she is all dressed up for a big evening out on the town.

1906. Tell her that she is pretty.

1907. If she loves dogs but can't have one, borrow one from a friend for a fun date in the park

1908. Rent out the party room in a restaurant for your own private dinner party.

1909. Hide small gifts along a path that you take her to walk along.

1910. Send a postcard of your town with a cute note saying that "home is where the heart is."

1911. Put your feelings in a display window of a local department store.

1912. Have your sentiments printed on plastic champagne glasses.

1913. Celebrate Mozart's birthday (January 27th) by making love to his music.

1914. Write a message on a frisbee and toss it over to her.

1915. Give him some travel games and puzzles the next time his company sends him away on an extended business trip.

1916. Read William Shakespeare's love poems to each other on his birthday (April 23rd).

1917. After she takes your name, send her monogrammed stationary with her new name.

1918. Have a star named for him by calling the International Star Registry at (800) 282–3333.

1919. If you have a winning instant lottery ticket, tuck it in her billfold the day of her big shopping expedition.

1920. Fill the glove compartment of her car with rose petals and love notes.

1921. Give books on love.

1922. Bake him an apple pie on Johnny Appleseed's birthday, September 26th.

1923. Celebrate her pet's birthday.

**1924.** Give him a copy of the newspaper from the day you first met.

**1925.** If she takes her lunch to work, give her a fancy lunch tote.

**1926.** If she is feeling a little homesick, make her a "family tree" by trimming a house plant with little photos of her relatives tied on with pretty ribbons.

**1927.** Present her with a lovely hat for the Kentucky Derby.

**1928.** Hang a horseshoe in his garage for good luck.

**1929.** Give him a six-pack of green beer on March 17th.

**1930.** Serve laughter and love along with each meal at the dinner table.

**1931.** Switch sides of the bed for a change.

**1932.** Dress up for a special evening at home together.

**1933.** Turn down the bed for her.

**1934.** When personal mail arrives that is addressed to both of you, wait to open it together.

---

*Always do right; this will gratify some people and astonish the rest.*
—MARK TWAIN

---

**1935.** Build a joint nest egg for a rainy day.

**1936.** Pour your heart into your relationship.

**1937.** Bolster each other's egos.

**1938.** Hibernate together on a freezing cold winter weekend.

**1939.** When making a wish while blowing out the candles on your birthday cake, wish for more romance in your relationship.

**1940.** Take a compatibility test to learn more about yourselves.

**1941.** Celebrate your own "Significant Other" day.

**1942.** Unplug the phone during romantic times.

**1943.** Share your two-stick popsicle.

**1944.** If you have to leave earlier than your mate to go to work on a cold winter morning, be a good duck and warm up his car.

**1945.** Take the scenic route when you are vacationing.

**1946.** Buy a soft and fluffy terry cloth towel large enough for two.

**1947.** Try sleeping in the spoon position.

**1948.** Touch often in nonsexual ways.

**1949.** Call on your lover for help during a crisis.

**1950.** Spend a lot of time alone together.

**1951.** Develop a shared hobby.

**1952.** During a power outage, make your own electricity.

**1953.** Find a good role model couple for your relationship.

**1954.** Take your relationship one day at a time.

**1955.** Do one nice thing for each other every single day.

**1956.** Ask your lover what she would like to change about you and try to accommodate her wish.

**1957.** Initiate new activities into your relationship.

**1958.** Once a month have a reconciliation day to tie up any loose emotional ends.

**1959.** Maintain an attractive and healthy weight.

**1960.** Give him your grandfather's pocket watch.

**1961.** Be polite.

**1962.** Rewrite your wedding vows to include what you have learned through the years.

**1963.** Think of yourselves as a team in the fun race of love.

**1964.** Enjoy all the added benefits of your mate's friendships.

**1965.** Involve your lover in your friendships

**1966.** Have a secret word and whenever anyone says it, kiss

**1967.** Write a love note in a foreign language and have fun watching your lover try to find out what it says.

**1968.** Squeeze into a photo booth and capture your silliness on film.

**1969.** Have a "Naked Day" (Adam and Eve started this).

**1970.** Enjoy a candlelight meal catered by Domino's.

**1971.** Treat yourselves on a cold rainy afternoon to chocolate fondue under warm covers.

**1972.** Share a recliner to watch a movie.

**1973.** Celebrate Hump Day every Wednesday.

**1974.** Try skinny dipping.

**1975.** Treat her to a mystery weekend where you do all of the planning and she just sits back and enjoys the festivities.

**1976.** Initiate sex.

**1977.** Have respect for what she does for a living

**1978.** Fully forgive each other after a really big argument.

**1979.** Speak softly when angry.

**1980.** Offer helpful solutions to her problems.

**1981.** Argue with your clothes off.

**1982.** Listen to Garth Brook's *If Tomorrow Never Comes*.

**1983.** De-fuzz all his favorite old sweaters.

**1984.** Say complimentary things about your mate to your family.

**1985.** Be the first one to offer a greeting.

**1986.** Talk happy talk around each other.

**1987.** Initiate kindness.

**1988.** Let him win at cards from time to time, even if you are a card shark.

**1989.** Inquire as to what is wrong when your mate looks sad.

1990. Write a romantic passage in every book you give.

1991. Tuck a love note in the medicine cabinet.

1992. Warm each other up on an Alaskan cruise.

1993. Carve your initials with an arrow through them in her desk drawer.

1994. Toast each other with a vintage wine from the year you met.

1995. Play hooky together.

1996. Send her love notes at her best friend's house.

1997. Take her on a dream shopping spree.

1998. Tolerate his mother.

1999. Serve dinner in bed.

2000. Buy her some heavy wool socks so that she won't get cold feet toward your relationship.

2001. Give a little gift the day before the big occasion.

2002. Read this book together!